THOMAS HARDY AND THE COSMIC MIND

THOMAS HARDY
AND THE COSMIC MIND

A NEW READING OF

THE DYNASTS

BY

J. O. BAILEY

CHAPEL HILL
The University of North Carolina Press

Copyright, 1956, by

The University of North Carolina Press

Manufactured in the United States of America

THIS BOOK WAS DIGITALLY PRINTED.

To

Doctor George Raleigh Coffman

Who taught me a great deal both inside the classroom and outside it

Preface

THOMAS HARDY brought to *The Dynasts* the fruit of some thirty years of intermittent meditation upon various plans for treating the Napoleonic wars in a dramatic or epic poem. He brought to the drama also a long-considered philosophic understanding of human life. This understanding perhaps governed Hardy's selection of historical materials, and it certainly informed his creation of the Spirits and their discussion of the Napoleonic struggle as a manifestation of the Immanent Will. The purpose of *Thomas Hardy and the Cosmic Mind* is to examine Hardy's drama, particularly in the light of his perusal of Eduard Von Hartmann's *Philosophy of the Unconscious*. Consideration of this book as an informing force in Hardy's own philosophy leads to examination of his interest in psychic phenomena, to a new interpretation of the Spirits in his drama, to reconsideration of the Immanent Will as Mind, to definition of Hardy's evolutionary meliorism, and to understanding his treatment of Napoleon as servant of the Will.

I use two editions of *The Dynasts* in this study, as a basic text the Pocket Edition issued in two volumes by Macmillan and Company of London in 1924; and for purposes of comparison, the edition issued in one volume by The Macmillan Company of New York in 1931. The American edition represents the earlier text, as it was printed from plates of editions published before 1910. In 1909, as a footnote in the Preface indicates, Hardy revised the poem for an edition of 1910, published in London. This revised edition provides the text for the standard library editions and for the Pocket Edition of 1924. I use the Pocket Edition instead of the Mellstock or the Wessex because it is easily available and texts are identical. Since references indicate Part, Act, and Scene, the phrases quoted may be easily found in any edition.

In *The Dynasts* Hardy had the speeches of the Spirits printed in italic type. He spelled *Napoleon* and *Josephine* with the French accent marks. Since it may be confusing to reproduce these typographical details in *Thomas Hardy and the Cosmic Mind,* I am ignoring them. The discussion includes frequent mention of the philosophic concept Schopenhauer called the "Will," Von Hartmann called the "Will" or the "Unconscious," and Hardy called, among other names, the "Will," the "Immanent Will," the "Unconscious," and the "Mind." Partly to avoid monotony and partly to be as precise as possible, I use the terms somewhat interchangeably, but with some intention of using the term that best fits the concept under discussion—thus, the *Will* when speaking of Its impulses and the *Mind* when speaking of Its thought. All three writers used the neuter pronoun *it* to refer to the Will; Hardy alone capitalized the word as *It*. I use *it* to refer to Schopenhauer's or Von Hartmann's Will, and *It* to refer to Hardy's. To avoid longwindedness, I frequently quote only a portion of a passage. I suppose it unnecessary, with this explanation, to use three periods to indicate an omission at the beginning or ending of a passage. Of course I indicate omissions within passages in the customary way. I hope that quoting fragments does not distort any meaning in relation to its context.

Dr. Lyman Cotten of the University of North Carolina very kindly read the manuscript and made a number of suggestions. Then I sent it to Dr. Carl J. Weber of Colby College. This noted Hardy scholar examined both the ideas and the writing with meticulous care and gave me unsparing advice that I have sought to heed in revision. I take this occasion of expressing a deep debt of gratitude to these good friends. I am grateful to the Trustees of the Hardy Estate, Macmillan and Company, Ltd., of London, and St. Martin's Press, Inc., of New York, for permission to quote as liberally as necessary from *The Dynasts*.

J. O. BAILEY

Chapel Hill, N. C.
April, 1956

Contents

	PAGE
Preface	vii
I Hardy and Psychic Phenomena "*The Universal Sympathy of Human Nature*"	1
II The Spirits "*Sources or Channels of Causation*"	33
III The Will as Mind "*What of the Immanent Will and Its Designs?*"	87
IV Hardy's Evolutionary Meliorism "*Consciousness the Will Informing*"	152
V Napoleon, Servant of the Will "*Such a Will I Passively Obeyed*"	182
Index	217

THOMAS HARDY AND THE COSMIC MIND

CHAPTER ONE

Hardy and Psychic Phenomena

"THE UNIVERSAL SYMPATHY OF
HUMAN NATURE"

THOMAS HARDY's *The Dynasts* differs from his novels of the 1890's in several ways. These novels express a pessimistic view of the world, but *The Dynasts* concludes with a paean of hope. The novels are realistic. Hardy's use of Spirits in *The Dynasts* follows a tradition of poetic drama, but it seems unrealistic that the Spirits speak to human beings who hear them and reply to them. In otherwise realistic scenes of the human action, strange and apparently psychic phenomena appear.

Using these phenomena, Hardy achieves sensational effects. The last scene of the historical drama, for example, is a conversation in a wood, at midnight, between Napoleon and Spirits. But examination of the phenomena reveals that they are more than the paraphernalia of Gothic tradition. They are developed in harmony with the view of the world that underlies *The Dynasts*. The concluding paean, in spite of many statements of determinism in the philosophic debate that runs through the drama, resolves the debate and forms a logical conclusion. Hardy meant this conclusion seriously. He expressed exasperation with critics who would not believe that he meant what *The Dynasts* says.

The differences between Hardy's views expressed in his later novels and the views that underlie *The Dynasts* stem from elements in his temperament, life-long interests, and reading in science and philosophy.

Hardy's temperament exhibits two main features. In thought he had much in common with the Spirit of the Years, who is presented as a stoic philosopher informed by science, but in feeling he had more in common with the compassionate Spirit of the Pities. His feeling attracted him toward the supernatural and the psychic. He "had a temperamental leaning towards the use of premonitions, omens, ghosts, and prophecies."[1] Hardy's most recent biographer, Evelyn Hardy, mentions elements of superstition in his temperament: "Like Cézanne he had a life-long dislike of being touched.

---

1. Ruth A. Firor, *Folkways in Thomas Hardy*, Philadelphia: University of Pennsylvania Press, 1931, p. 304.

Possibly he felt, as the painter did, that others had the power of drawing strength from him by physical contact. . . . Such fastidiousness, a characteristic of highly reserved, sensitive people, appears in Hardy's case, to have been rooted in superstition."[2]

His authorized biography, Mrs. Hardy's *The Early Life* and *The Later Years*,[3] contains evidence that Hardy was temperamentally drawn toward the supernatural. Hardy helped prepare the material for this biography, selecting from his notebooks and journals what he wished to include. In view of the many interests of his life, he selected a surprising number of notations about the supernatural, observations of psychic puzzles, and speculations in this area. For example, his journal for March 5, 1890, records "a curious instance of sympathetic telepathy." In a train on the way to London, Hardy wrote "the first four or six lines of 'Not a line of her writing have I,'" about a woman's death.[4] The journal adds, "The woman whom I was thinking of—a cousin—was dying at the time, and I quite in ignorance of

2. Evelyn Hardy, *Thomas Hardy: A Critical Biography*, London: Hogarth Press, 1954, p. 40.
3. Florence Emily Hardy, *The Early Life of Thomas Hardy*, New York: Macmillan, 1928, and *The Later Years of Thomas Hardy, 1892-1928*, New York: Macmillan, 1930.
4. See "Thoughts of Phena at News of Her Death," Thomas Hardy, *Collected Poems*, New York: Macmillan, 1943, p. 55.

it."[5] Though Hardy may have made many of his notes originally for use in stories, his selecting them for his biography, after his stories were written, suggests that he thought they threw light on himself.[6]

Hardy discussed psychic experiences with various people. William Archer quotes Hardy as saying to him in 1901: "My mother believed that she once saw an apparition. A relative of hers, who had a young child, was ill and told my mother that she thought she was dying. My mother laughed at the idea; and as a matter of fact she apparently recovered, and went away to her home at some distance. Then one night —lying broad awake as she declared—my mother saw this lady enter her room and hold out the child to her imploringly. It afterwards appeared . . . that she died at that very time;

---

5. *The Early Life*, p. 293.

6. These notes include the story of the architect Hicks, who dreamed a dream that came true "exactly as he had beheld it in his dream" (*The Early Life*, p. 61); the story of a dumb woman who suddenly spoke to prophesy the French Revolution and then dropped dead (*ibid.*, p. 165); the story of Conjurer Mynterne, who accurately prophesied a man's unexpected death (*ibid.*, pp. 220-221); the story of Dr. Anna Kingsford's helping Mr. E. Maitland write a book by supplying him with sentences she had dreamed as he worked on the book (*ibid.*, pp. 234-235); the story of a member of the Savile Club whose wraith appeared on the streets while the man remained in the club (*ibid.*, pp. 277-278); the story of Hardy's dog's strange behavior in apparent foreknowledge of a Mr. Watkins's death (*The Later Years*, p. 241); and the story of Hardy's own observation of a "dark man" standing by Mrs. Hardy at a tea, though she was certain no such man was there (*ibid.*, p. 259).

but the odd thing was that, while she was sinking, she continually expressed a wish that my mother should take charge of the child."[7]

On the other hand, though Hardy was not credulous of the ordinary spooky tale, he included a number of such tales in his biography.[8] This fact seems to indicate that Hardy was temperamentally fascinated by the supernatural and the psychic. Perhaps his poem "A Sign Seeker" best expresses both his fascination and his skepticism:

> I have lain in dead men's beds, have walked
> The tombs of those with whom I had talked,
> Called many a gone and goodly one to shape
>   a sign,
> And panted for response. But none replies;

[7] William Archer, "Real Conversations. Conversation 1.—With Mr. Thomas Hardy," *The Critic*, XXXVIII (April, 1901), 309-318; the passage quoted is from p. 313.

[8] He included a story told by the Reverend C. Holder of a local man who "saw a dark figure with a cloven foot" toss a drunken ecclesiastic onto a horse. But Hardy considered this story "rather well-found than well founded." (*The Early Life*, p. 203.) He included a "variant of the superstitions attached to pigeon's hearts" used in witchcraft, but the word *superstition* indicates his attitude (*ibid.*, p. 266); the story of a farmer with a "blasting" eye that injured his own cattle and was treated by a "conjurer or white witch" (*ibid.*, pp. 268-269); the details of spell-working by two girls who so injured a young man that the girls were sent to prison (*The Later Years*, p. 11); and a comment upon Vagg Hollow, where "'things' used to be seen," where horses would not go unless whipped, and where a wagoner saw "smoke and a hoofed figure" rise from a "wool-pack in the middle of the road" (*ibid.*, p. 96). This note on Vagg Hollow seems to underlie the poem "Vagg Hollow," *Collected Poems*, p. 614.

> No warnings loom, nor whisperings
> To open out my limitings,
> And Nescience mutely muses: When a man
>   falls he lies.[9]

Hardy speculated about the reality of matter. He wrote in his journal for February 13, 1887: "I was thinking a night or two ago that people are somnambulists—that the material is not the real—only the visible, the real being invisible optically. That it is because we are in a somnambulistic hallucination that we think the real to be what we see as real."[10] In 1901, when he was working on *The Dynasts*, he wrote in a letter that he did not send: "My own interest lies largely in non-rationalistic subjects, since non-rationality seems, so far as one can perceive, to be the principle of the Universe. By which I do not mean foolishness, but rather a principle for which there is no exact name, lying at the indifference point between rationality and irrationality."[11]

Both Hardy's temperamental fascination and his speculation are reflected in his novels, stories, and poems.[12] Yet it is curious that among the hundreds of instances in which supernatural or psychic forces are suggested, no charac-

---

9. *Collected Poems*, p. 44.
10. *The Early Life*, p. 243.
11. *The Later Years*, p. 90.
12. Since Firor, *Folkways in Thomas Hardy*, treats the point, it need not be developed here.

ter in Hardy's novels sees an outright ghost. Hardy's stories present visions, dreams of wraiths and incubi, psychic influences, and the strange knowledge of conjurers, but they are not ghost stories. Often a psychic influence may be rationally explained. Mr. South's death when a tree is cut down in *The Woodlanders* may be explained as autohypnotism. As Guerard remarks of this story, "Hardy's psychosomatic notions provide some of his most curious pages."[13] These notions seem to express belief—Guerard says that Hardy "did believe literally"—"in the imagination's effective power over matter—in the power of the mind to effect bodily changes, in the telepathic fascinating power of the strong mind over the weak."[14] The story "The Withered Arm" is an instance of Hardy's use of this psychokinesis.[15]

13. Albert J. Guerard, *Thomas Hardy: The Novels and Stories*, Cambridge: Harvard University Press, 1949, p. 106.
14. *Ibid.*, p. 92.
15. Rhoda Brook dreams of the incubus of her rival, Gertrude, and in the dream hurls the incubus to the floor, wrenching its left arm. Gertrude's arm withers, with livid marks like those of Rhoda's fingers. Hardy's Preface to *Wessex Tales* says that in the tale from which he made the story, the incubus did not appear in a dream at night, but appeared while Rhoda was "lying down on a hot afternoon." Hardy says, "To my mind the occurrence of such a vision in the daytime is more impressive than if it had happened in a midnight dream." (New York and London: Harper and Brothers, 1912, p. viii.) Hardy's comment suggests a measure of temperamental half-belief. Perhaps his choice of the dream was not deliberate; he had forgotten

Hardy had no university education to channel his thought away from unorthodox speculation. Perhaps for this reason he turned his attention all the more curiously to various frontiers of knowledge. He acquired in late adolescence some acquaintance with the fatalism of Greek drama. Then he read Darwin with the shock and the conversion to agnosticism explicit in his biography and his early poem "Hap." He read the works of Huxley, Spencer, and J.S. Mill. These men wrote with confidence that the scientific method and reason were solving some of the problems of matter and life, but they also indicated mysteries beyond the scope of Victorian science. In reading the works of scientists and rationalists, Hardy certainly pondered theories concerned with these mysteries. He observed a Victorian arena filled with attacks upon Darwin's theory, not only by opponents of evolution, but also by evolutionists like Samuel Butler, who favored the Lamarckian principle of vitalism or evolution guided by a Life Force. Perhaps these facts, along with some nostalgia for his lost religious faith and other elements in his temperament, prompted

---

some details of the original. But this choice matches his measure of half-belief with a measure of reluctance to portray the incubus as a fact, even in fiction.

Hardy to look for some Prime Cause behind the "Crass Casualty" of "Hap."[16]

Then, in the late 1880's, Hardy "came under the powerful sway of that line of great thinkers whose first and most illustrious name is that of Plato, whose first representative in modern times is Berkeley, and whose viewpoint is later championed and developed by Kant, Fichte, Hegel, and Schopenhauer."[17] Schopenhauer's influence is evident in Hardy's novels from the time of *The Woodlanders* (1887) onward. Certainly significant echoes of Schopenhauer's doctrines appear in *The Dynasts*. Indeed, several dissertations and books have been written to demonstrate that *The Dynasts* is an illustration of Schopenhauer's philosophy.[18]

But I believe that many of the ideas traced to Schopenhauer in studies of *The Dynasts* reflect Schopenhauer's thought as modified by a later philosopher, Eduard Von Hartmann, whose *Philosophy of the Unconscious*[19] Hardy

16. *Collected Poems*, p. 7.
17. Ernest Brennecke, Jr., *Thomas Hardy's Universe: A Study of a Poet's Mind*, London: T. Fisher Unwin, 1924, p. 21.
18. See, for example, Helen Garwood, *Thomas Hardy: An Illustration of the Philosophy of Schopenhauer*, Philadelphia: Winston, 1911 (University of Pennsylvania doctoral dissertation), and Brennecke, *Thomas Hardy's Universe*.
19. Eduard Von Hartmann, *Philosophy of the Unconscious* (authorised translation by W. C. Coupland), London: Paul, Trench, Trübner, & Co., 1884, 3 vols. The edition of 1890 is quoted in this study.

was reading as he planned *The Dynasts*. Hardy stated that "My pages show harmony of view with Darwin, Huxley, Spencer, Comte, Hume, Mill, and others, all of whom I used to read more than Schopenhauer."[20] Hardy told Miss Helen Garwood that his philosophy was "a development from Schopenhauer through later philosophers."[21] The statement sounds like a reference to Von Hartmann, for the *Philosophy of the Unconscious* discusses Schopenhauer's philosophy at length and is to a large extent a development from it.

The development exhibits the fundamental difference that the entity Schopenhauer calls Will, Von Hartmann calls the Unconscious. Hardy was perhaps prepared to accept Von Hartmann's concept by his earlier reading in Mill. Rutland says that Mill may have been the first to suggest to Hardy that the Prime Cause may be an unconscious Mind. Mill said, "That nothing can *consciously* produce Mind but Mind is self-evident, being involved in the meaning of the words; but that there cannot be *unconscious* production cannot be assumed."[22]

20. Carl Jefferson Weber, *Hardy of Wessex: His Life and Literary Career*, New York: Columbia University Press, 1940, p. 203.
21. Garwood, p. 11.
22. Quoted by William R. Rutland, *Thomas Hardy: A Study of His Writings and Their Background*, Oxford: Basil Blackwell, 1938, p. 69, from John Stuart Mill's "Theism." Rutland discusses this point fully.

Hardy's Immanent Will is exhibited as Unconcious Mind. And the development exhibits another significant difference. Nothing in Schopenhauer's doctrines suggests the meliorism that is expressed in the paean of hope at the conclusion of *The Dynasts*. Quite the contrary! Critics have even tended to deny that Hardy meant this conclusion seriously because they have not found it consistent with Schopenhauer. Brennecke, for example, states of Hardy's meliorism that "this—quite anti-Schopenhauerian—idea is not expressed as a conviction, but is only tentatively advanced as the forlorn hope of the irrational Pities."[23] Simply, these critics have not read the drama in the light that Von Hartmann's *Philosophy of the Unconscious* throws upon Hardy's Immanent Will and Its processes.

Meanwhile, both before and after reading Von Hartmann, Hardy talked with scientists and others who might throw light on psychic phenomena. His journal for October 23, 1894, records a conversation at the Savile Club with the biologist Sir Edwin Ray Lankester on the subject of "hypnotism, will, etc." Hardy records that Lankester "did not believe in silent influence, such as making a person turn round by force of will without communication. But

23. Brennecke, *Thomas Hardy's Universe*, p. 144.

of willing, for example, certain types of women by speech to do as you desire—such as 'You *shall*, or you *are to*, marry me,' he seemed to have not much doubt. If true, it seems to open up unpleasant possibilities."[24] Lankester's "not much doubt" and Hardy's "If true" suggest that Hardy was more skeptical than the scientist, but that he puzzled over the problem.

When William Archer talked with Hardy in 1901, at the time that Hardy was working on *The Dynasts*, and recorded the "real conversation," the talk circled about psychic phenomena and their relation to science and philosophy. Hardy said:

I quite admit the pitiful ineffectualness, even grotesqueness, of all the alleged manifestations of the spirit world, and the eeriness of spirits, to our seeming —. . . I don't know that the grotesqueness, the incompleteness of the manifestations is at all conclusive against their genuineness. Is not this incompleteness a characteristic of all phenomena, of the universe at large? It often seems to me like a half-expressed, an ill-expressed idea. Do you know Hartmann's Philosophy of the Unconscious? It suggested to me what seems almost like a workable theory of the great problem of the origin of evil,—though this, of course, is not Hartmann's own theory,—that there may be a consciousness, infinitely far off, at the other end of the chain of phenomena, always striving to express itself,

24. *The Later Years*, p. 34.

and always baffled and blundering, just as the spirits seem to be.²⁵

Hardy's phrases "a workable theory of the great problem of the origin of evil" and "a consciousness . . . at the other end of the chain of phenomena, always striving to express itself" provide a key to Hardy's meaning in *The Dynasts*. Archer must have quoted Hardy accurately, for these phrases illuminating *The Dynasts* were published while Hardy was still working on Part First.

Hardy's discussion of psychic phenomena led him to mention Von Hartmann's *Philosophy of the Unconscious* as a book apparently fresh in his mind. There is some question about when Hardy read this book. *Die Philosophie des Unbewusstes* was published in 1868, but Hardy did not read German with ease. It was translated into English by W. C. Coupland, and the translation was published in 1884. Thereafter numerous editions appeared. Blunden says that Hardy owned the edition of 1893.²⁶ In 1901, the book came naturally into Hardy's conversation with Archer. The Preface of *The Dynasts*, which is dated September, 1903, says that "on a belated day about six years back, the following drama was outlined, to be taken up

25. Archer, p. 316.
26. Edmund Blunden, *Thomas Hardy*, London: Macmillan and Co., 1942, p. 182.

now and then at wide intervals ever since." (P. viii)[27] Apparently Hardy's "six years back" refers to the final design of *The Dynasts,* rather than to notes on the Napoleonic wars he had been making for some thirty years; and the final design reflects, from the Fore Scene to the last line, the influence of Von Hartmann. It seems likely, then, that Hardy had read the *Philosophy of the Unconscious* by 1897[28] and that he had it freshly in mind in 1901. Possibly he reviewed it or referred to it from time to time all during his composition of *The Dynasts.*

The *Philosophy of the Unconscious,* in three long and difficult volumes, undertakes to review critically all the sciences and philosophies known to the mid-nineteenth century, as a basis for Von Hartmann's special contribution. The discussion ranges from Newton to Darwin, and from Plato to Schopenhauer, with a great deal of both exposition and criticism of the ideas of Darwin and Schopenhauer. Von Hartmann adopts Schopenhauer's view that the basic Reality or Thing-in-Itself is the Will, but he

27. Thomas Hardy, *The Dynasts: An Epic-Drama of the War with Napoleon,* Pocket Edition, London: Macmillan and Co., 1948 (Vol. I) and 1949 (Vol. II), reprint of the edition of 1924. I am placing references to this edition of *The Dynasts* in the text.

28. Purdy agrees that Hardy "outlined and commenced the composition of *The Dynasts* as we know it" in 1897. Richard Little Purdy, *Thomas Hardy: A Bibliographical Study,* London, New York, Toronto: Oxford University Press, 1954, p. 122.

conceives the Will as unconscious mental Energy. He calls it indifferently the Will and the Unconscious. He traces the operation of the Unconscious through the phenomena it inhabits, both living and non-living. He finds that the impulses of living matter called instinct are processes of the Unconscious. He writes of the development of consciousness in man and perhaps the higher animals as an accident in evolution—a result of the thrust of the Unconscious toward self-realization. Consciousness derives ideas or concepts, besides the impulses from the Unconscious, from sense-stimuli. Von Hartmann surmises that conscious beings may, with some difficulty, choose to act in accordance with concepts so derived, rather than in response to impulses from the Unconscious. At the present stage of human development, the impulses of the Unconscious usually control human behavior, but Von Hartmann surmises that as consciousness continues to develop, it may become the controlling factor and might react upon the Unconscious, for it is immanent in its parts. These features of Von Hartmann's theory are reflected in *The Dynasts*. Many details of Von Hartmann's theory reflected in Hardy's drama are pointed out in the following chapters.

It would be possible to suppose that Hardy read Von Hartmann and made use of his system for artistic purposes without belief in the system, much as he used the material of folklore in his novels. But the evidence indicates that Hardy believed Von Hartmann's ideas to be an approach to truth. The novels and poems contain many suggestions that before writing *The Dynasts* Hardy had given up belief in any discoverable purpose in the universe and had adopted a determinism somewhat like that expressed by the Spirit of the Years, or at best had seen in the gloomy philosophy of Schopenhauer the most acceptable explanation for phenomena. Yet the nostalgic tone of many statements expressing skepticism or pessimism[29] suggests that he did so unhappily. Then Hardy found that the second chapter of the *Philosophy of the Unconscious* opens with a promise that science and philosophy can restore the concept of purpose that these studies had seemed to deny. Chapter II opens with: "One of the most important and familiar manifestations of the Unconscious is Instinct, and the conception of Instinct rests on that of Purpose."[30] The chapter continues with a complex mathematical

---

29. See, for instance, "The Impercipient," *Collected Poems*, pp. 59-60, and "In Tenebris," pp. 153-155.
30. Von Hartmann, I, 43.

demonstration of this statement. Whether Hardy followed the formulas and the reasoning based on them may be doubted, but he must have found mathematical demonstration of what he wanted to believe impressive. *The Dynasts* reflects enough from Von Hartmann's *Philosophy* to indicate that Hardy did not turn the leaves casually; he seems to have studied the book. It will be shown that Hardy intended the ideas of *The Dynasts* to be taken seriously, but one cannot take them all seriously—one cannot understand all of Hardy's meaning—without reading some passages in the light of Von Hartmann's prose exposition of the idea. It seems likely that Hardy read the *Philosophy of the Unconscious* as thoughtfully as he had read *The Origin of Species* many years before. To him, for he was no professional scientist or philosopher, Von Hartmann's interpretation and criticism of the sciences and philosophies of his time may have seemed wholly valid. In a letter quoted by Rutland, Hardy mentions Von Hartmann in a connection that indicates reliance upon him as a thinker. Hardy wrote, of an essay in Maeterlinck's *Le Temple Enselevi*: "Far be it from me to wish to disturb any comforting phantasy, if it be barely tenable. But alas, no profound reflection can be needed to detect the sophistry in M. Maeterlinck's argument, and to see that the original difficulty recognised by thinkers like Schopenhauer, Hartmann, Haeckel, etc., and by most of the persons called pessimists, remains unsurmounted."[31]

Hardy mentions Haeckel. The distinguished German biologist Ernst Haeckel published in 1899 a semi-philosophical résumé of scientific learning at the end of the nineteenth century. The book was translated into English and published as *The Riddle of the Universe* in 1900.[32] Hardy's biographers agree that he read this book; Hardy mentions Haeckel with respect, as in the quotation above, and in a headnote to the poem cites Haeckel as one of the sources for his poem "Panthera."[33] Several passages in *The Dynasts*, to be cited later, seem to reflect Hardy's reading of *The Riddle of the Universe*. It expresses a thoroughgoing determinism and possibly, aside from passages that can be paralleled, gave shape to the determinism expressed by the Spirit of the Years.

Both Von Hartmann and Haeckel define their point of view as monistic and repeatedly

31. Rutland, p. 68.
32. Ernst Haeckel, *The Riddle of the Universe at the Close of the Nineteenth Century* (translated by Joseph McCabe), London: Watts and Co., 1900. The edition of 1901 is quoted in this study.
33. *Collected Poems*, pp. 262-268. The story told in "Panthera" is found on p. 336 of Haeckel, *The Riddle of the Universe*.

declare that monism is the view held by informed thinkers. Von Hartmann says that "Wherever we may look among the original philosophical or religious systems of the first rank, everywhere do we meet with the tendency to Monism. . . . and only the shallowest religions and philosophical systems have rested contented with an external dualism."[34] He continues that "we have seen in all philosophies of the modern epoch this tendency to Monism."[35] And he states that the acceptance of monism is important for society: "Precisely in our own time, when the opposition between the unmediated extremes of a rigid *theistic dogmatism* and an *irreligious atheistic naturalism* is threatening to become more irreconcilable, the golden mean of a *spiritualistic Monism or Pantheism,* which supplies both parties with a bridge for mutual understanding and union on neutral soil, appears to be of the highest importance for the peaceful spiritual development of modern society."[36]

Haeckel, in his "Author's Preface," asserts that his monism is based upon the evidences of science: "my Monistic philosophy . . . is the

34. Von Hartmann, II, 234.
35. *Ibid.*, II, 239.
36. *Ibid.*, II, 271. The italics are Von Hartmann's. Von Hartmann italicizes many words and phrases. Throughout this study, I am italicizing exactly as in the texts quoted.

complete expression of the conviction that has come to me, after many years of ardent research into Nature and unceasing reflection, as to the true basis of its phenomena."[37] He states it as an understood fact that informed people accept monism, saying that "we have returned to that monistic attitude which our greatest realistic poet, Goethe, had recognised from its very commencement to be alone correct and fruitful."[38]

These passages seem to underlie Hardy's implication in the Preface of *The Dynasts* that he is a monist and his statement that "The wide prevalence of the Monistic theory of the Universe forbade, in this twentieth century" the use of epic machinery taken from mythology.[39]

37. Haeckel, p. xiii.
38. *Ibid.*, p. 20.
39. Hardy does not define his particular type of monism. *The Dynasts* seems to indicate that he believed matter to be more a *product* of the Mind than an aspect of It, for matter is able to impede It. Brennecke says that Schopenhauer's "world-view is Idealistic Monism." Tracing Hardy's concept to Schopenhauer, he says: "That Hardy's world-view also is Idealistic Monism is evidenced by the frequency with which the epithet 'Immanent' is applied to the Will. . . . Hardy usually employs . . . the term 'Immanent,' because he is primarily interested in excluding every conception of an exterior force essentially different from the universe and outside of it." (*Thomas Hardy's Universe*, p. 66.) Probably this statement is close to the truth. Von Hartmann spoke of "the golden mean of a *spiritualistic Monism*" in the passage quoted above. But Hardy seems to use the term *monism* in a fluid way. The context in the Preface of *The Dynasts* suggests that he intends to contrast monism with religious and mythological dualism, say, God *versus* Satan. Perhaps Hardy's concept of a Mind that needs the teaching and help of Its creatures stems from Mill's

(P. viii) Hardy defines his Will as "the First or Fundamental Energy," (P. ix) and this concept of the Will as energy reflects, if it does not necessarily derive from, Haeckel's statement of this idea. Haeckel says, "Mechanical and chemical energy, sound and heat, light and electricity, are mutually convertible; they seem to be but different modes of one and the same fundamental force or *energy*. Then follows the important thesis of the unity of all natural forces, or, as it may also be expressed, the 'monism of energy.' "[40]

The concept of the Fundamental Energy as mental, an Unconscious, but at least Mind, undergirding and permeating all phenomena and manipulating them through impulses, opens up the possibility of entirely natural, but as yet mysterious, forces. In spite of Hardy's temperament, his "longing to discern more than natural agency behind and in the senseless revolution of things,"[41] he did not believe in the ghostly-supernatural. In the conversation with Archer, Hardy said:

---

idea of a struggling God, to which Hardy added ideas from Comte, Schopenhauer, and Von Hartmann. See John Stuart Mill, *Three Essays on Religion: Nature, The Utility of Religion, and Theism*, London: Longmans, Green, etc., 1874, and Hardy's poetry, for instance, "God's Education," *Collected Poems*, p. 261.

40. Haeckel, p. 260.
41. Guerard, p. 98.

I am most anxious to believe in what, roughly speaking, we may call the supernatural—but I find no evidence for it! ... For instance, I seriously assure you that I would give ten years of my life ... to see a ghost,—an authentic, indubitable spectre.

W. A. And you have never seen one?

Mr. Hardy. Never the ghost of a ghost. Yet I should think that I am cut out by nature for a ghost-seer. My nerves vibrate very readily; people say I am almost morbidly imaginative; my will to believe is perfect. If ever ghost wanted to manifest himself, I am the very man he should apply to. But no—the spirits don't seem to see it.

Archer then contended, perhaps as devil's advocate, that if ghosts are incredible, perhaps one may go so far toward the supernatural as belief in telepathy. He told Hardy that "there seems to be ample evidence for the existence of forms of cerebral energy not as yet measured and catalogued. . . . don't you think there is very fair evidence for the possibility of thought-transference . . . ?" Hardy replied, "No. In all the researches of the Psychical Society, I find nothing that carries conviction." Thus, while the conversation circled about ghosts and such evidences for telepathy as the Psychical Society recorded, Hardy's attitude was negative.

Then Archer likened the processes of telepathy to "Röntgen-ray images" and "wireless telegraphy" and asked: "is it inconceivable that the human brain may prove to be a more powerful and more sensitive receiver than any invented by Marconi or Tesla . . . ?" At this analogy with scientifically understood processes, Hardy said, "I quite admit that all this is conceivable—that there is nothing in it which contradicts the very laws of thought. . . . I merely repeat my demand for evidence! Have you known, in your own experience, an instance of thought-transference?" Archer could give no instance from his experience, but Hardy (reversing his field) gave an instance and then evaluated it: "For example, the thoughts of a relation of mine used to 'jump with' mine in a way not easily to be explained by mere coincidence. It would often happen that, after a long silence, both of us, in the same breath, would speak of some person or thing apparently quite absent from the thoughts of either five minutes before. . . . the thing used to occur (or so I thought) too frequently to be always accounted for [as a 'train of association']. However, I admit—or rather this is my very point—that the instance is too trifling, and too uncertain, to have the smallest evidential value."[42]

Thus Hardy did not believe in ghosts and in the autonomous power of the human mind to transmit and receive messages without using

42. Archer, pp. 313-314.

some sensory medium. He did not believe in the ghostly-supernatural. But belief in the supernatural—generally a part of dualism—is not the same as belief in the manipulation of the human mind by impulses from the Will, for in monism the Will is the one Energy and Its "pulsions" (as Hardy called them) are everywhere. In *The Dynasts*, the Spirits in communication with human beings are "channels of Causation" between the Will and man. *The Dynasts* does exhibit apparent telepathy between human characters, as in the spread of rumors, but such rumors seem to be vibrations of the Will-webs. In short, *The Dynasts* is full of psychic phenomena, but they are treated as natural, of the same order, say, as instinctive behavior; and they are "conceivable" within the concept of the Unconscious—the Will as mental Energy. Perhaps Hardy himself best summed up the distinction in a letter to Dr. W. C. Saleeby in 1915: "Half my time—particularly when writing verse—I 'believe' (in the modern sense of the word) . . . in spectres, mysterious voices, intuitions, omens, dreams, haunted places, etc., etc. But I do not believe in them in the old sense of the word any more for that."[43] If I understand Hardy's distinction between the "old sense" of *believe* (faith, trust, as in God)

43. *The Later Years*, p. 168.

and the "modern sense" (intellectual assent), when he was writing poetry Hardy was able to create and use supernatural phenomena to which he gave intellectual assent as symbols for some underlying, invisible Reality, but he did not believe these symbols for Reality to be knowable, sensible, ponderable facts.

But there can be no reasonable doubt of Hardy's intellectual assent to the Will of *The Dynasts*, which he sought to portray as a Reality. In the Preface he rejects as a basis for representation of the Overworld the orthodox or Miltonic symbols and those used in mythology because they do not represent tenable concepts. He sought symbols consistent with monism and suitable to express a modern outlook. He suggests that his readers "look through the insistent, and often grotesque, substance at the thing signified." (Pp. viii-xi)

The grotesqueness belongs to the "alleged manifestations of the spirit world" and the "eeriness of spirits, to our seeming." But, in the conversation with Archer, Hardy stated that grotesqueness is not "at all conclusive against their genuineness," and he immediately mentioned the *Philosophy of the Unconscious* and the possibility that a consciousness "at the other end of the chain of phenomena" may be striving to express itself. Von Hartmann discusses this possibility in ways to be examined in Chapter Four. Aside from the concept of the Will as the Unconcious, it seems the most significant idea Hardy derived from Von Hartmann. It is one basis of the meliorism that forms the climax and the central meaning of *The Dynasts*.

Hardy must have meditated somewhat independently and at length on this idea in order to give it poetic expression. At any rate, though always acknowledging the basis in the concept of the Unconscious, he stated, after his reading of Von Hartmann may have become dim, that the idea was his own. A letter to Edward Wright on June 2, 1907, states his belief in the philosophic pattern of *The Dynasts* and claims that the meliorism of the play is his "own idea solely." The letter says:

> In a dramatic epic . . . some philosophy of life was necessary, and I went on using that which I had denoted in my previous volumes of verse (and to some extent prose) as being a generalized form of what the thinking world had gradually come to adopt, myself included. That the Unconscious Will of the Universe is growing aware of Itself I believe I may claim as my own idea solely—at which I arrived by reflecting that what has already taken place in a fraction of the whole (*i. e.* so much of the world as has become conscious) is likely to take place in the mass; and there being no Will outside the mass—that is, the Universe—the

whole Will becomes conscious thereby: and ultimately, it is to be hoped, sympathetic.[44]

Hardy's basic faith was certainly in science, but he obviously regarded the *Philosophy of the Unconscious* as a semi-scientific work, not inconsistent with science at the frontiers beyond evidence and demonstration. He regarded Von Hartmann's speculation about the development of consciousness in the Unconscious as tenable. He developed this speculation in his own mind to the point where he even thought he had originated it.[45] He knew that speculation of this kind goes beyond demonstrable science and cautious rationalism, but he was willing to go there. He also knew, of course, that the particulars of his poetic drama, however consistent with a philosophic principle, could not be consistent with particulars in a far-off future. He took refuge in declaring himself an irrationalist

44. *Ibid.*, pp. 124-125. Hardy repeats the claim in a letter to "My Dear Clodd" of February 20, 1908: "The idea of the Unconscious Will becoming conscious with flux of time, is also new, I think, whatever it may be worth. At any rate I have never met with it anywhere." (*Ibid.*, p. 276.) He states it yet again in a letter to Dr. Caleb Saleeby on December 21, 1914: "But I think the view of the unconscious force as gradually *becoming* conscious: *i.e.* that consciousness is creeping further and further back towards the origin of force, had never (so far as I know) been advanced before *The Dynasts* appeared." (*Ibid.*, p. 270.)

45. Apparently Hardy did add an important, original idea to the material he found in Von Hartmann. The nature of his contribution is more fully discussed in Chapter Four.

and admitting inconsistencies. On February 18, 1920, Mrs. Hardy wrote for him a reply to Joseph McCabe, saying, "He says he thinks he is rather an irrationalist than a rationalist, on account of his inconsistencies."[46] Hardy, I think, created the phenomena of *The Dynasts* in accordance with scientific theory as far as it explains Reality, and then relied on philosophic speculation and even feeling for particulars beyond this point.

Hardy's biography records his exasperation when reviewers misunderstood his machinery and refused to take his ideas in *The Dynasts* seriously. In one memorandum he wrote: "If, instead of the machinery I adopted, I had constructed a theory of a world directed by fairies, nobody would have objected, and the critics would probably have said, 'What a charming fancy of Mr. Hardy's!' But having chosen a scheme which may or may not be a valid one, but is presumably much nearer reality than the fancy of a world ordered by fairies would be, they straightway lift their brows."[47]

Time has passed since the reviewers found themselves out of their depth in Hardy's philosophy. Recent critics and biographers agree that Hardy meant *The Dynasts* to express a ten-

46. *The Later Years*, pp. 209-210.
47. *Ibid.*, p. 104.

tative and poetic, but none the less tenable, view of the world. In 1931, McDowall called the conclusion of *The Dynasts* "genuinely part" of Hardy's thought, and his meliorism "an outlet from the oppression of an unconscious universe which he felt to be his own, and original."[48] Rutland's more detailed discussion in 1938 commented upon the conclusion of Part First, Act V, Scene iv, "the passionate debate between the Pities and the Years upon the problem of suffering," saying that it "must be considered one of the most significant utterances in the literature of the last fifty years. In less than fifty lines, Hardy here not only expresses the central theme of *The Dynasts* . . . he also reveals the history of his own soul; how his revulsion from the intolerable injustice of useless suffering drove him to seek in philosophy an intellectual explanation. . . . the significance of this page far transcends that of any one school of thought, and even that of Hardy himself; because it is universal."[49] In 1942, Blunden's biography asserted that the Immanent Will gave objective form to Hardy's sincere belief: "he therefore based his *Dynasts* in a First Cause other than that of the churches, meaning this with all his might if ever he meant anything."[50]

48. Arthur McDowall, *Thomas Hardy: A Critical Study*, London: Faber and Faber, 1931, p. 169.
49. Rutland, p. 315.   50. Blunden, p. 229.

Yet Hardy insists in his Preface that the doctrines of *The Dynasts* are but tentative views. The doctrines of the Spirits "are but tentative, and are advanced with little eye to a systematized philosophy warranted to lift 'the burthen of the mystery' of this unintelligible world. The chief thing hoped for them is that they and their utterances may have dramatic plausibility enough to procure for them, in the words of Coleridge, 'that willing suspension of disbelief for the moment which constitutes poetic faith.' " (P. viii) The Preface of his last volume of poetry, *Winter Words*, says essentially the same thing: "I also repeat what I have often stated on such occasions, that no harmonious philosophy is attempted in these pages—or in any bygone pages of mine, for that matter."[51] Of his works as a whole, Hardy says, "I have repeatedly stated in prefaces and elsewhere that the views in them are *seemings*, provisional impressions only, used for artistic purposes," for "they represent approximately the impressions of the age, and are plausible, till somebody produces better theories of the universe."[52] These statements do not say—Hardy never said—that he did not seriously mean the doctrines of *The Dynasts*.

51. Thomas Hardy, *Winter Words*, New York: Macmillan, 1928, p. vi.
52. *The Later Years*, p. 175.

Hardy intended to set forth in this poetic drama a "tentative," "provisional," and "plausible" theory of the universe, without pretending to be a systematic philosopher or to accept a philosopher's responsibility. This intention has been generally respected by his critics. Abercrombie said that the philosophic poetry of *The Dynasts* means "all 'philosophical' poetry can mean. It must give certain *shape* to an aesthetic metaphysic, formulate in clear art some supposed relation of known and unknowable, whereby man may live. But there is no necessity that the formulation, the metaphysic, should have to submit itself to a strictly philosophic scrutiny."[53] Of Hardy's statements that he did not attempt a systematic philosophy, Duffin says, "Such disclaimers are appended by implication to every 'philosophy' emanating from a person over the age of eighteen and not a professional philosopher." Yet, Duffin continues, "We must, I think, be allowed to infer from impression and opinions constantly and (in fact) consistently voiced something of the mind and outlook behind them."[54]

53. Lascelles Abercrombie, *Thomas Hardy: A Critical Study*, New York: Kennerley, 1912, p. 153.
54. Henry Charles Duffin, *Thomas Hardy: A Study of the Wessex Novels, The Poems, and The Dynasts*, Manchester: University Press, 1916. The edition quoted is the third edition, 1937, p. 337.

Writing to express a scientifically informed, modern view of the world, Hardy wrote to express also his feelings as a man and a poet. His feelings—his compassion, even his yearning for religion—qualify his intellectual position in important ways. His medium of poetic drama allowed him to use Spirits as spectators, interpreters of the action, and impersonated points of view. The Spirits also take part in the dramatic action as "sources or channels of Causation."

CHAPTER TWO

The Spirits

"SOURCES OR CHANNELS OF CAUSATION"

THE SPIRITS of *The Dynasts* bear the stamp of Hardy's thought and temperament. Yet it blurs one's understanding of the drama to read it with the idea that the impressive views of any one Spirit express all that Hardy means. It is common to view the Spirit of the Years alone as spokesman for Hardy. "There is no doubt," says one critic, "that what the ancient Spirit of the Years says is what Mr. Hardy thinks."[1] Ideas expressed by this Spirit do reflect a part of Hardy's thought, as ideas expressed by Hamlet reflect a part of Shakespeare's. But to understand *The Dynasts*, it is necessary to understand each of the Spirits as a character and then to observe the role he plays in the drama.

A chorus of the Spirits says, "Our readings Why and Whence,/Are but the flower of Man's

1. W. L. Courtney, "Mr. Thomas Hardy and Aeschylus (II)," *Fortnightly*, CVII (1917), 629-640; p. 633.

intelligence," (I, VI, viii, 137)² and Hardy's Preface suggests that the Spirits are "sources or channels of Causation." (P. viii) These statements should help us see what Hardy's Spirits mean and what function they serve in the drama.

Some light is thrown on the Spirits by observing their relation to a tradition of poetic drama. Scholars have pointed out that the lyric choruses of Aeschylus, Goethe, Shelley, Hugo, and Swinburne contributed features of Hardy's Choruses of Spirits.³ Fairchild recently pointed out a fact of which no hint is given in Hardy's biographies, that Robert Buchanan's *The Drama of Kings* (1871)—which Hardy seems to have read about 1889—provided Hardy an immediate suggestion for development of his Spirits. Buchanan's Chorus "philosophically . . . is a crude preliminary sketch of the Pities" of Hardy's drama;[4] his Chorus divides into Semichoruses; and his "*ancient* Shadow men call Time" has the "hoary weariness and disillusion" of Hardy's Spirit of the Years.[5]

---

2. I am using a shorthand notation for references to the play: "I, VI, viii, 137" means Part First, Act VI, Scene viii, page 137.

3. See, for example, William R. Rutland, *Thomas Hardy: A Study of His Writings and Their Background*, Oxford: Basil Blackwell, 1938, p. 289.

4. Hoxie N. Fairchild, "The Immediate Source of *The Dynasts*," PMLA, LXVII (March, 1952), 43-64; p. 58.

5. *Ibid.*, p. 54.

THE SPIRITS

But the facts pointed out about the patterns Hardy observed throw light chiefly on his machinery. Hardy uses Choruses, but not all of them mean what the Chorus means, for example, in Buchanan's *The Drama of Kings*—the voice of the author. Most of Hardy's Choruses are groups of Spirits of one kind or another, and each says in song what the Spirit indicated might say in verse or in prose. The Chorus of the Years, for example, speaks for the Spirit of the Years in a lyric mood. This fact is true even when a Chorus breaks into Semichoruses; the Semichoruses sing in lyric parts what the Spirit they represent might say. For example, during the battle of Austerlitz, Semichorus I of the Pities begins a prayer to the "Great Necessitator" to dull the suffering of the soldiers; Semichorus II continues the prayer, with a restatement of the plea. (I, VI, iii, 118) Sometimes Semichoruses even continue the same sentence. Semichoruses of Ironic Spirits, telling the evolutionary story for the Spirit of the Pities' benefit, continue a single sentence through six stanzas—three by Semichorus I and three by Semichorus II, between the opening of the sentence and the period. (I, VI, iii, 119) In short, the purpose of the Choruses and the Semichoruses is somewhat like the purpose of the "aerial music" that frequently accompanies their songs: to express in music an idea that the Spirit represented might have spoken.

Yet we may suppose that each General Chorus speaks for Hardy. Since the Spirits debate issues that are not resolved till the end of the drama, General Choruses are not frequent: the drama contains only four Choruses that I identify as General. A "General Chorus of Intelligences" concludes the Fore Scene. Stating the mystery of the Will, this Chorus obviously speaks for Hardy. A "Chorus of Intelligences" has a single line, in comment upon Napoleon's "Anon to England," at the end of Act III of Part First, singing: "If Time's weird threads so weave." The Chorus must speak for Hardy here. A Chorus that is not labeled "General," but that evidently includes in its "we" all the Spirits, concludes Part First. This Chorus speaks of the Spirits as "the flower of Man's intelligence," which is itself an "incident/Of the all-urging Will." This statement echoes Hardy's Preface. Then the After Scene ends with a Chorus that follows two sets of Semichoruses, sung by the Spirits of the Years and of the Pities. Like the Chorus ending Part First, it seems to be a Chorus of all the Spirits, though not so named in either place. If so, the climactic statement of evolutionary meliorism in the final Chorus states what all the Spirits mean

THE SPIRITS

and therefore, I believe, what Hardy means.[6]

Besides suggestions for his Choruses, no doubt Hardy did find in Buchanan's play the seed for his Spirits who are described as Intelligences; Buchanan has "strange Intelligences" as "Celestial Spectators."[7] But Hardy found only the seed in Buchanan; he nourished it with his own thought and the philosophical and scientific books he read. The ideas Hardy's Spirits express owe little if anything to Buchanan; they are his own.

Hardy's Preface states what he intends his Spirits to be: "It was thought proper to introduce, as supernatural spectators of the terrestrial action, certain impersonated abstractions, or Intelligences, called Spirits. They are intended to be taken by the reader for what they may be worth as contrivances of the fancy merely." Then Hardy explains the extent to which the doctrines of the Spirits represent tentative but plausible views of the world. He says of the clash of opinion among the Spirits, "In point of literary form, the scheme of contrasted Choruses and other conventions of this external feature was shaped with a single view to the

6. Of course Choruses stating facts about the action state what Hardy means, whoever the singers. Other songs in the play are labeled simply Chorus, but each seems to me a union of Semichoruses just preceding. Hardy's inconsistent labeling of his Choruses seems to me an oversight.

7. Fairchild, pp. 53-54.

modern expression of a modern outlook, and in frank divergence from classical and other dramatic precedent which ruled the ancient voicings of ancient themes." (Pp. viii-ix) Thus the contrasted points of view expressed by the Spirits are those held tenable by informed modern minds.

In the Fore Scene the Spirit of the Years states the function of the Spirits as spectators: "Our scope is but to register and watch/By means of this great gift accorded us—/The free trajection of our entities." (P. 2) This scope embraces the fundamental questions of the meaning, direction, and purpose of life.

The activities of the Spirits in their communications with the human characters have puzzled Hardy's critics. Abercrombie says that "The economy of the poem is injured by them; for in a poem so persistently elaborating a universal necessity, how can they be anything but patently superfluous? The action cannot go otherwise than it does; human and superhuman effort can never alter it or make its course more certain, can never do aught but carry out the inevitable."[8] Rutland also says that the intervention of the Spirits in human affairs is "philosophically incongruous . . . for if, as we are re-

8. Lascelles Abercrombie, *Thomas Hardy: A Critical Study*, New York: Kennerley, 1912, pp. 187-188.

THE SPIRITS

peatedly told, every detail of the action is part of the predetermined mechanics of Immanent Will, the Phantoms described as personifications of Sympathy and Passionless Insight have no business to interfere with them; nor, by the premises, have they any power to do so."[9]

These comments assume that what the Spirit of the Years says of "universal necessity" expresses Hardy's conviction. But the poem as a whole questions determinism and suggests the possibility of influences upon human life from other sources than the Will. Even if determinism be granted, the interventions of the Spirits are not "philosophically incongruous." The Spirits are channels of Causation, the strings, so to speak, that lead from the puppet-master Will to the human marionettes.

Hardy refers to the Spirits as "sources or channels of Causation" in a sentence in which he rejects "Divine personages from any antique Mythology" to serve these purposes. (Preface, p. viii) In using the word *channels*, Hardy was evidently thinking of the supernatural figures used in epic poetry to express or execute the will of God or of the gods. The phrase indicates that his Spirits also act as intermediaries between the Will and the human characters. The Will operates directly as impulses so with-

9. Rutland, p. 317.

in the mind that the mind itself seems to originate them. From time to time, Hardy exhibits the Will acting in this way. His problem was how to show Its impulses in continuous operation. To picture the Will as always on the stage as puppet-master manipulating every action would be clumsy. A spectator at a marionette show does not see the manipulator; he sees only the seemingly living figures in motion and perhaps now and then the strings that move their limbs. Hardy wished to remind his readers that the puppet-master Will is always there by keeping the strings, so to speak, constantly in view. The Spirits as channels for the "pulsions" of the Will remind us that the impulses are continuous. When the Spirits speak to men, the human characters do not see the Spirits; they seem to hear voices within themselves. We, observing both the show and the machinery, think of the Force behind the scenes.

When the Spirit of the Years whipers to Nelson, he conveys the message of the Will, which Nelson hears within himself. Nelson says:

> And I have warnings, warnings, Collingwood,
> That my effective hours are shortening here;
> Strange warnings now and then, as 'twere within me,
> Which, though I fear them not, I recognize!
> (I, II, i, 39)

THE SPIRITS

The Spirit makes it clear that his messages of this kind do not originate with him; he is but an agent of the Will. When the Spirit of the Pities chides him because he "racks" Villeneuve, the Spirit of the Years says:

> I say, as I have said long heretofore,
> I know but narrow freedom. Feel'st thou not
> We are in Its hand, as he?—Here, as elsewhere,
> We do but as we may; no further dare.
> (I, II, ii, 43)

The Spirits, then, when they take part in the human action, are usually channels of the Will.

The Spirits also act independently now and then, as *sources* of Causation, in response to their own reflections and feelings, and even in resistance to the Will. When the Spirit of the Pities speaks to Napoleon, for instance, he symbolizes an impulse from consciousness as opposed to the unconscious Will. This matter is involved with the freedom of the will, discussed in Chapter Four. These dramatized projections of the Will and of other influences are not inconsistent, within Hardy's peculiar theory of the Will as unconscious Mind.

Besides acting as sources or channels of Causation, the Spirits are spectators of the drama of the Napoleonic war and of the operation of the Will. They discuss and explain motives. They act as narrators to sum up scenes that might clutter the stage if presented in action. Their comments provide transitions from scene to scene. Able to see into the future, they prophesy and whisper presentiments of death. Sometimes they serve Hardy's purposes in the manner of Gothic portents to deepen the reader's apprehension.

In these activities, no one of the Spirits reflects all of Hardy, though the doctrines of the Spirit of the Years seem to reflect his typical thought; the Spirit of the Pities, his feeling and temperament. But the Spirit of the Years does not speculate beyond the ground of reasoned experience. Hardy does. The Spirit of the Years, therefore, does not fully represent Hardy. The same is true for each of the Spirits.

The Spirit of the Years is the leader of the Spirit band. He undertakes to answer the question asked by the Shade of the Earth as the Fore Scene opens: "What of the Immanent Will and Its designs?" As the curtain rises on the human drama, he invites the other Spirits to observe the play: "Hark now, and gather how the martial mood/Stirs England's humblest hearts. Anon we'll trace/Its heavings in the upper coteries there." (I, I, i, 8) That Hardy should have a Spirit as showman and usher and that his name might be Years were perhaps suggested to Hardy by a speech of Time in Buchanan's *The Drama of Kings*: "I/Am Time and most eternal. I am he,/God's Usher, and my duty it is to lead/The actors one by one upon the scene."¹⁰ The Spirit of the Years, if not like Time "most eternal," is called "Eldest-born of the Unconscious Cause." (I, II, ii, 42) He has lived many centuries, back to the "germ of Being" (Fore Scene, p. 2) and refers to events before man appeared. The Spirit of the Years is showman not only for the human drama, but for the Will. Ironic Spirits call him "Showman Years," (II, V, vi, 281) and in this role he has, among his "antique privileges," that of exhibiting the Will. As he does so in the Fore Scene, he says:

> As key-scene to the whole, I first lay bare
> The Will-webs of thy fearful questioning;
> For know that of my antique privileges
> This gift to visualize the Mode is one. (P. 6)

The Spirit Sinister calls the Spirit of the Years, as showman of the Will, "Its official Spirit." (I, VI, viii, 137) But like all the Spirits as channels of Causation, the Spirit of the Years is Its "slave." He says, "I am but an accessory of Its works,/Whom the Ages render conscious; and at most/Figure as bounden wit-

10. Robert Buchanan, *The Drama of Kings*, London: Strahan & Co., 1871, p. 17.

ness of Its laws." (I, I, ii, 15)[11] Of all the Spirits, he says, "Its slaves we are: Its slaves must ever be." (I, VI, viii, 137)

In the first version of *The Dynasts*, Hardy's Preface defined the Spirit of the Pities, but said of all the other Spirits, including the Spirit of the Years, that they are "eclectically chosen auxiliaries whose signification may be readily discerned."[12] Perhaps the fact that critics tended to regard the Spirit of the Years alone as spokesman for Hardy moved him to add in 1909 a definition of this Spirit and his Choruses: "Another group [than the Pities] approximates to the passionless Insight of the Ages." (P. ix) Hardy's phrase "passionless Insight" suggests that the Spirit of the Years may be characterized primarily as a stoic.[13] The Spirit calls himself an aloof observer of life from its beginning. Watching its processes, he remains unperturbed, saying: "Though, as for me,/I care not how they shape, or what they be." (Fore Scene, p. 3)

11. In the first version, "Whom the Ages render conscious" is given as "Whom chance has rendered conscious." The revision suggests that by 1909 Hardy had a somewhat stronger feeling for purpose in the development of consciousness. See Thomas Hardy, *The Dynasts: A Drama of the Napoleonic Wars*, New York: The Macmillan Company, 1944 (reprint of edition of 1931 that used plates made before the edition of 1910), p. 24. This edition is hereafter called the American edition.

12. American edition, p. viii.

13. I am grateful to Dr. Carl J. Weber for this suggestion that the Spirit of the Years may be characterized as primarily a stoic and for several other suggestions concerned with the Spirits.

THE SPIRITS

Charged with having little sense of mercy, the Spirit of the Years states:

> Mercy I view, not urge;—nor more than mark
> What designate your titles Good and Ill.
> 'Tis not in me to feel with, or against,
> These flesh-hinged mannikins Its hand upwinds
> To click-clack off Its preadjusted laws;
> But only through my centuries to behold
> Their aspects, and their movements, and their mould. (Fore Scene, p. 4)

He speaks again of his "unpassioned essence" that cannot be stirred by men's sufferings. (I, II, iii, 17) He looks with equanimity upon death, and in prophesying the death of Fox speaks of "my good friend Death." (II, I, ii, 152) Though he is to some extent moved by the end of the drama, the Spirit of the Years is still resolved not to "let raptures rule" his sober thought. (After Scene, p. 524)

Evidently the stoic aspects of the Spirit's character reflect important parts of Hardy's thought. Hardy admired the stoic Marcus Aurelius. His journal for December 31, 1885, quotes from this philosopher, as a relief from his own sadness: "This is the chief thing: Be not perturbed; for all things are according to the nature of the universal."[14] Hardy quotes from these lines again in *Tess of the D'Urber-*

14. *The Early Life*, p. 231.

villes,[15] and yet again in the poem "Rome: The Vatican."[16] Blunden concludes his biography of Hardy with the quotation and Hardy's statement, "The foregoing is one passage, among others, that I have had much in mind."[17]

One foundation for the stocism in Hardy's thought was his reading in the sterner works of literature. Rutland points out that the Spirit of the Years likewise knows these works. The Spirit "rebukes the Spirit Sinister as 'Thou Iago of the incorporeal world.' He says to Napoleon, after his stumble at the Niemen, 'The portent is an ill one, Emperor;/An ancient Roman would retire thereat!' More impressively, he quotes Latin in the wood of Bossu: 'Sic diis immortalibus placet'—/Thus is it pleasing to the immortal gods,/As earthlings used to say.' "[18]

Another foundation for the stocism in both Hardy's thought and the experience of the Spirit of the Years is a scientific understanding of the world. The Spirit has observed universal process through all time, and he sets human life against the backdrop of the universe as it was

---

15. Thomas Hardy, *Tess of the D'Urbervilles*, Harper's Modern Classics edition, New York and London: Harper and Brothers, not dated, p. 331. See Chapter XXXIX in any edition.
16. *Collected Poems*, p. 94.
17. Edmund Blunden, *Thomas Hardy*, London: Macmillan and Co., 1942, p. 280.
18. Rutland, p. 336.

known to Victorian scientists. The Spirit regards Christianity as a "local cult" insignificant among the "systems of the suns" that with their "planet train" sweep on "In mathematic roll unceasingly." (I, I, vi, 33) The human race itself he calls "earthlings"; men are, in comparison with many forms of life, "extemporary/And transient." (I, III, i, 61) Of course he has observed the processes of evolution. Semichoruses of Ironic Spirits sing that "He of the Years beheld, and we,/Creation's prentice artistry," and then tell the story of evolution. (I, VI, iii, 119) At the end of the drama, when all the Spirits have been stirred by the events of the Napoleonic wars, the Spirit of the Years places the great struggle in astronomic perspective. It is "but one flimsy riband" of the "web Enorm,/Whose furthest hem and selvage may extend/To where the roars and plashings of the flames/Of earth-invisible suns swell noisily." (After Scene, pp. 521-522)

Like many a Victorian scientist, the Spirit of the Years is a determinist. Though Hardy's bent toward determinism is evident in his novels, it seem likely that Hardy intended the Spirit of the Years to express the determinism of such a scientist as Haeckel. Reading Haeckel's *The Riddle of the Universe* while he was working on *The Dynasts*, Hardy found many passages like the following: "The great struggle between the determinist and the indeterminist, between the opponent and the sustainer of the freedom of the will, has ended to-day, after more than 2,000 years, completely in favour of the determinist. . . . We now know that each act of the will is as fatally determined by the organisation of the individual and as dependent on the momentary condition of his environment as every other psychic activity."[19] The Spirit of the Years' similar determinism is everywhere evident, as in this song of Choruses of the Years:

> Ere systemed suns were globed and lit
> The slaughters of the race were writ,
> And wasting wars, by land and sea,
> Fixed, like all else, immutably! (I, II, v, 53)

Haeckel rejects Christianity, and his "after more than 2,000 years" seems to refer to pre-Christian and Christian phases of belief in freedom of the will and hence in sinful man's responsibility. The Spirit of the Years treats the doctrine of original sin as a myth and rejects it as justification for the ways of the Will:

> Some, too, have told at whiles that rightfully
> Its warefulness, Its care, this planet lost

---

19. Ernst Haeckel, *The Riddle of the Universe at the Close of the Nineteenth Century* (translated by Joseph McCabe), London: Watts and Co., 1900, pp. 133-134.

> When in her early growth and crudity
> By bad mad acts of severance men contrived,
> Working such nescience by their own device.—
> Yea, so it stands in certain chronicles,
> Though not in mine. (Fore Scene, p. 2)

In his "personal" life the Spirit of the Years exhibits calm compassion. When Pitt is dying, this Spirit, who has "communed with that intelligence" many a time, refuses to speak to him of further disaster: "Nay, I have spoke too often! . . ./Now I would leave him to pass out in peace,/And seek the silence unperturbedly." (I, VI, viii, 136-137) In the songs preceding the battle of Waterloo, a Chorus of the Years joins a Chorus of the Pities in lamenting the disaster to the dumb creatures of the field:

> The mole's tunnelled chambers are crushed by wheels,
> The lark's eggs scattered, their owners fled;
> And the hedgehog's household the sapper unseals.
> The snail draws in at the terrible tread.
> (III, VI, viii, 483)

Throughout the drama, the Spirit of the Years speaks of war with bitterness; he scolds the Spirit Sinister for his cruelty; and in the wood of Bossu, he flays Napoleon. In the After Scene, the Spirit of the Years confesses that he once, in youth, dreamed the dreams that inspire the Pities, and apparently he joins in the Chorus of hope that ends the drama.

The Spirit of the Years has a marked gift of prophecy. When Pitt speaks in the House of Commons, the Spirit prophesies Pitt's death and his future fame. Again, when Pitt makes his last speech, after Trafalgar, the Spirit of the Years says that:

> his last large words,
> As I may prophesy—
> . . . .
> Will spread with ageing, lodge, and crystallize,
> And stand embedded in the English tongue
> Till it grow thin, outworn, and cease to be.
> (I, V, v, 104)

He prophesies likewise that the name of Rostopchin, Governor of Moscow, "will ring/Far down the forward years uncannily!" (III, I, vi, 346) When hints reach England that Napoleon is quarreling with Alexander, the Spirit of Rumour asks the Spirit of the Years' permission to enter the throng at Carlton House and confirm the rumor. The Spirit of the Years says, "I'll go," and enters the hall "in the shape of a pale, hollow-eyed gentleman wearing an embroidered suit," and there prophesies the Franco-Prussian war, the death of Perceval, the fall within five years of "The rawest Dynast of the group concerned," and the settlement by which

"Europe's mouldy-minded oligarchs" will "Be propped anew." As statesmen gape, the Spirit "passes into the crowd and vanishes." No one can identify him. Castlereagh says, "His manner was that of an old prophet, and his features had a Jewish cast, which accounted for his Hebraic style." (II, VI, vii, 320-321) When Marie Louise parts with Napoleon, the Spirit of the Years prophesies uncertainly—"to use/ The bounded prophecy I am dowered with"— that she will not see him again. (III, IV, ii, 401) His "bounded prophecy" represents the Spirit's reading of the Will—"So is't ordained by That Which all ordains" (I, V, v, 104)—and perhaps also his "passionless Insight" and ancient experience that enable him to extend causes into their conjectural results. In some areas, the Spirit of the Years cannot prophesy; he distrusts, for example, the quite accurate prophecies of the Spirit of the Pities, based upon feeling.

That the Spirit of the Years' prophecy is "bounded" is consistent with other limitations. His knowledge (except his prophecies) is limited to the facts of experience. He insists, concerning the future, that "old Laws operate yet," but admits that "Already change/Hath played strange pranks since first I brooded here." (Fore Scene, p. 3) Since answers to fundamental questions in the drama, "Why and Whence?" lie outside the ground of experience, it cannot be said that the Spirit of the Years' conclusions represent fully either answers to the questions of *The Dynasts* or Hardy's view of the world.

The proposition for which the Spirit of the Years stands in the clash of opinion among the Spirits is stated on the second page of the Fore Scene:

> In the Foretime, even to the germ of Being,
> Nothing appears of shape to indicate
> That cognizance has marshalled things terrene,
> Or will (such is my thinking) in my span.
> Rather they show that, like a knitter drowsed,
> Whose fingers play in skilled unmindfulness,
> The Will has woven with an absent heed
> Since life first was; and ever will so weave.

The other propositions that he states and defends derive from this one.

The speeches of the Spirit of the Years "have an austere and sometimes rugged grandeur" that makes "an impression out of all proportion to their actual length in the text."[20] This fact may account for the frequently expressed opinion that the Spirit of the Years is Hardy's spokesman. He does seem to represent the stoic and scientific part of Hardy's thought.

20. Rutland, p. 335.

Perhaps Hardy originally conceived the Spirit of the Pities as the most important of the Spirits. To the extent that Hardy found suggestions in Buchanan's *The Drama of Kings*, it is significant that Buchanan's Chorus, expressing the author's views, "is a crude preliminary sketch of the Pities." The Spirit of the Pities is the only Spirit Hardy described individually in the original Preface of *The Dynasts*. There a sentence singles out the Spirits of the Pities and lumps the rest together: "These phantasmal Intelligencies are divided into groups, of which one only—that of the Pities—approximates to 'the Universal Sympathy of human nature—the spectator idealized' of the Greek Chorus, the remainder being eclectically chosen auxiliaries whose signification may be readily discerned."[21] Or perhaps Hardy thought that his readers might most easily misunderstand the Spirit of the Pities because, representing human nature, the Spirit wavers in his hopes and fears. At any rate, in his revision of 1909, Hardy added a clause to the description of the Spirit to call attention to his inconsistency and explain it. After the word *Chorus*, he inserted: "it is impressionable and inconsistent in its views, which sway hither and thither as wrought on by events." (P. ix)

21. American edition, p. viii.

The Spirit of the Pities is inconsistent, and Hardy's clause states exactly why. To some extent, the Spirit is one of the "sources or channels of Causation," but he does not always transmit the message of the Will. The Will is unconscious; the Spirit of the Pities is affected by the sensations from which consciousness is formed. He receives impulses from perception of suffering; he is "wrought on by events." He feels intensely, sometimes to the point of agony or hysteria; and as a *source* of impulse he tries to inspire unselfish acts—in *resistance* to the Will. He protests unconscious Process, and throughout the drama seeks to awaken men, the other Spirits, and even the Will to awareness and compassion.

Presumably Hardy supposed that consciousness reflective enough to oppose the Will is unique in man. Where the Spirit of the Years is ancient, the Spirit of the Pities is as young on the geologic scale as mankind. At the height of one protest against the "very sorriness" of the Will, the Spirit of the Years says sneeringly of the younger Spirit's attitude: "Affection ever was illogical," and the Spirit Ironic says of the Spirit of the Pities: "How should the Sprite own to such logic—a mere juvenile—who only came into being in what the earthlings call their Tertiary Age!" (I, I, vi, 36-37) This remark

THE SPIRITS

echoes in tone and phrase Haeckel's statement of man's origin: "The youngest and most perfect twig of the branch primates is man, who sprang from a series of man-like apes towards the end of the Tertiary period."[22] Throughout the play, the other Spirits treat the Spirit of the Pities as an innocent or an upstart. When he prays to the Will to ease the suffering at Austerlitz, a Chorus of Ironic Spirits addresses a Chorus of the Pities as "Innocents" and sings the story of what happened in the world "Ere ye, young Pities, had upgrown." (I, VI, iii, 118-119) Now and then the Spirit of the Pities does act like a schoolboy. Lectured by the Spirit of the Years for supposing he could affect the Will, he gives the lesson back when the Spirit of the Years wishes he could move the Will to enchain the Spirit Sinister: "Would thou couldst!/But move That scoped above percipience, Sire,/It cannot be!" (I, I, vi, 35) Such is man, perhaps, bruised, compassionate, now and then courageous, faltering, sometimes childish.

As the Spirit of the Years is showman of the Will, the Spirit of the Pities is showman of human suffering. In the function of reporting events, the Spirit of the Years reports facts, but the Spirit of the Pities the feelings about facts.

22. Haeckel, p. 14.

He is moved by any scene of pain, mental or physical. When Villeneuve is torn between his conscience and Napoleon's command, the Spirit of the Pities observes his feelings and interprets them to the Spirit of the Years (and, of course, the reader): "He pens in fits, with pallid restlessness,/Like one who sees Misfortune walk the wave,/And can nor face nor flee it." The difference between the way the Spirit of the Pities sees the man's agitation and the Spirit of the Years observes what the man is doing is clear in the Spirit of the Years' reply. He states the fact that Villeneuve is writing a letter to Decrès and is having trouble with "Words that go heavily!" (I, II, ii, 40)

Perhaps the Spirit of the Pities roughly corresponds to the hero of epic poetry who must descend into Hell to find light or salvation. The only Hell in Hardy's modern, monistic universe is the suffering in men's minds and bodies. The Hell into which the Spirit of the Pities descends as epic-hero is suffering man. He does so willingly, and invites the Spirit of the Years to join him, so that he may win this Spirit to feel sympathy for man. Proposing to the Spirit of the Years that they sit in the gallery of Commons as visitors and listen to the debate, the Spirit of the Pities says:

THE SPIRITS 57

> Let us put on and suffer for the nonce
> The feverish fleshings of Humanity,
> . . . .
> So may thy soul be won to sympathy
> By donning their poor mould. (I, II, iii, 17)

The Spirit of the Pities grew up, according to a Chorus of Ironic Spirits, "From out the deep where mortals moan/Against a ruling not their own." (I, VI, iii, 119) As a spectator of the human drama, he is spokesman for suffering man. Hardy uses him to describe the suffering from the fever on Walcheren Island. The Spirit of the Pities says, "We catch a lamentation shaped thuswise," and a Chorus of the Pities sings the touching and terrible lament of the dying soldiers. (II, IV, viii, 251) Though, in reporting the scenes of battles, other Spirits describe the strategic movements and the clash of armies, the Chorus of the Pities does not sing of these or of the heroic leaders. It sings of the exhausted men. At Talavera the Spirit of the Pities describes the soldiers of both sides coming "In homely need" to drink at a little rill and grasping hands across it before they die. (II, IV, iv-v, 243-246) Again, when the Spirit of the Years commands the Spirit of the Pities to report the battle of Albuera "and what you witness say," the Spirit of the Pities speaks of "red smears upon the sickly dawn," and of "Mixt nationalities . . ./ Wheeling . . ./In moves dissociate from their souls' demand,/For dynasts' ends that few even understand!" The Spirit of the Years, impatient at this focus upon men's feelings, demands the facts, and the Spirit of Rumour takes over to present the movements of the troops. The Spirit of the Pities interrupts the Spirit of Rumour to express something that seems to him important: "Wrecked are the ancient bridge, the green spring plot,/The blooming fruit-tree, the fair flower-knot!" (II, VI, iv, 299-300) For the Spirit of the Pities' feeling extends beyond the pain of man, and even of animals, to man's home laid waste, the work of his hands destroyed, and the flowering, fruitful earth blighted. Before Waterloo, a Chorus of Pities sings so poignantly of the destruction of the field—"The green seems opprest, and the Plain afraid"—that a Chorus of the Years picks up the song, and even a Chorus of Sinister Spirits adds a stanza to lament the dead! (III, VI, viii, 483-484)

The Shade of the Earth calls the Spirit of the Pities "Cordial One." (Fore Scene, p. 3) Because the Spirit, as this term suggests, looks for truth in the heart, rather than the mind, he sees all the action differently from the other Spirits. Undoubtedly Hardy thought of the saying that life is a tragedy to those who feel, but a comedy to those who think, when he had the Spirit of the Pities speak of "this terrestrial tragedy," and the Spirit Ironic interrupt with "Nay, comedy." (Fore Scene, p. 4) This contrast in the Fore Scene indicates that Hardy intended to establish the fact that the Spirit of the Pities' values are different from the values of the others. Seeing through the lens of feeling, judging with the criteria of the heart, this Spirit has a message for the Spirits who are blinded by the glare of reason.

Like the Spirit of the Years, the Spirit of the Pities has some power of prophecy, but its source seems to be less insight into the Will or extension of causes into consequences than insight into the heart—insight of the kind hardheaded men call "woman's intuition." The Spirit of the Pities foresees events concerned with the feelings that are not foreseen by the Spirit of the Years, who does not understand how he does so and calls the prophecy "guess." As Napoleeon thinks of attacking Austria, the Spirit of the Pities, fore-feeling that Napoleon will wed Maria Louisa, says:

> Has he no heart-hints that this Austrian court,
> Whereon his mood takes mould so masterful,
> Is rearing naïvely in its nursery-room
> A future wife for him?

The Spirit of the Years says, "Thou dost but guess it,/And how should his heart know?" (II, III, ii, 213) The same difference of view is repeated when the Spirit of the Pities foresees the death of Sir John Moore in a vision, seeing "A filmy outline like a monument,/Which yet is but the insubstantial air." The Spirit of the Years replies, as a husband might reply to an intuitive wife, "Read visions as conjectures; not as more." (II, III, iii, 216) But Sir John dies in the following battle! The Spirit of the Pities foresees Napoleon's Grand Army, marching into Russia, "returning in a chattering flock/Bleached skeletons." (III, I, i, 330) With the Spirit of the Years, he sees the phantoms of death that dance before the officers who leave the Duchess of Richmond's ball for Waterloo.

Informed by the suffering in man's "poor mould" and moved by compassion and values the other Spirits do not see, the Spirit of the Pities questions and challenges their reading of the world. When the Spirit of the Years scolds him because he does not "heed the Cause of things" and futilely seeks to influence Napoleon, the Spirit of the Pities replies, "I feel, Sire, as I must!" (I, I, vi, 36) He makes no progress toward converting the Spirits to his point of view so long as he relies on feeling alone, but begins to influence them when he supports his feeling with logic. Through the drama, the Spirit of the Pities grows in experience and assurance. He sloughs off mere sentimentality. His temperament would draw him toward anything romantic, but he learns to resist the lure. As Ney's cavalry advances at Waterloo, the Spirit of the Pities is caught up in admiration of the theatrical spectacle of "Red lancers, green chasseurs: behind the blue/The red" and the troopers "each with the air/Of one who is himself a tragedy." But his experience has taught him better, and he concludes that the technicolor show is only a "barbaric trick." (III, VII, iv, 495-496)

The Spirit of the Pities believes in freedom of the will. Because he is "wrought on by events," as well as manipulated by the Will, he sees that there are two sources of impulse and decision, and believes that one may choose. In the Fore Scene the Spirit of the Years speaks sneeringly of the Spirit of the Pities' belief; the Spirits will watch:

> the spectacle of Europe's moves
> . . . as [if] they were self-ordained
> According to the naïve and liberal creed
> Of our great-hearted young Compassionates.
> (P. 6)

This problem of freedom of the will is discussed in Chapter Four.

In the clash of opinion among the Spirits, the Spirit of the Pities supports the proposition stated by the Chorus of the Pities that Hardy used instead of a General Chorus to close Part Second. Answering a Chorus of the Years that has described the Will as a "rapt Determinator . . ./That neither good nor evil knows!" the Chorus of the Pities sings:

> Yet It may wake and understand
> Ere Earth unshape, know all things, and
> With knowledge use a painless hand,
>   A painless hand! (II, VI, vii, 322)

That is, the Spirit of the Pities supports evolutionary meliorism. Semichoruses of the Pities, developing this proposition, lead into the final Chorus of the drama that seems to express Hardy's meaning.

That the Spirit of the Pities expresses Hardy's positive message seems clear in Hardy's letters, discussed in Chapter One. To the extent that Hardy drew upon Von Hartmann, we may observe that the Spirit of the Pities' idea of making the Will moral and just by making It aware of suffering is suggested in the *Philosophy of the Unconscious*. Von Hartmann says, "Thus not *in itself* can moral action have a value for the Unconscious, but only so far as it lessens the sum of the sorrow to be felt by it. . . . Although, therefore, morality and jus-

THE SPIRITS

tice, *as such,* cannot be ends in the world-process, they might well *be so for the sake of happiness,* if this, as an object directly concerning the essence of the Unconscious, may be regarded as end, which might well be supposed."[23] Some critics agree that the Spirit of the Pities (more than the other Spirits) represents Hardy. Rutland, for example, points out that Hardy's quotation from Schlegel, in describing the Spirit of the Pities as "the Universal Sympathy of human nature," is taken from a passage that speaks of the Chorus as "the incorporation into the representation itself of the sentiments of the poet."[24] Rutland also says that the Spirits of the Pities "are the inevitable outcome of, and climax to, Hardy's growing quarrel with the 'sorry scheme of things,' which finds vent with progressive violence in the later novels."[25] Hardy's latest biographer, Evelyn Hardy, seems exactly right in saying that the Spirit of the Pities represents Hardy's "intense compassion, which embraced, not only, the 'feverish fleshings of humanity,' but the flora and fauna of the battlefield, so tenderly that we grieve with the poet for the standing corn which will never be cut."[26]

23. Von Hartmann, II, 365. 24. Rutland, p. 330.
25. *Ibid.,* p. 338.
26. Evelyn Hardy, *Thomas Hardy: A Critical Biography,* London: Hogarth Press, 1954, p. 285.

Hardy does not describe the other Spirits in his Preface, but speaks of them all as "auxiliaries whose signification may be readily discerned." In the cast of characters Hardy listed the Spirits Sinister and Ironic in the same bracket. This fact has doubtless led critics to lump these Spirits together and treat them both as evil. Comments like the following are typical: The "Spirits Sinister and Ironic . . . deserve perhaps the title of evil."[27] The "Spirits Sinister and Ironic . . . are opposite to the Spirit of the Pities."[28] "It is the business of . . . the Spirits Ironic and Sinister to jeer and make satirical remarks."[29] But, whatever Hardy may have intended when he wrote out the cast of characters, examination of the Spirit Ironic's character and his role in the drama indicates that these views are wrong.

The Spirit Ironic is more closely associated with both the Spirit of the Years and the Spirit of the Pities than with the Spirit Sinister. He does have Mephistophelian traits, similar to those of the "Mephistophelian visitants" in Hardy's novels.[30] But Hardy's characters of

27. Harold Child, *Thomas Hardy*, London: Nisbet and Co., 1916, p. 104.
28. Thomas H. Dickinson, "Thomas Hardy's 'The Dynasts,'" *North American Review*, CXCV (April, 1912), 533.
29. Courtney, p. 633.
30. J. O. Bailey, "Hardy's 'Mephistophelian Visitants,'" *PMLA*, LXI (December, 1946), 1146-1184. At the time I wrote

this kind, like Diggory Venn in *The Return of the Native*, were reasoners, rather than evil men. Perhaps Hardy's impulse to create a rationalistic Mephistopheles and to associate him with the Spirits of the Years and of the Pities was supported by a passage in the *Philosophy of the Unconscious*. Von Hartmann wrote: "Philosophy is hard, cold, and insensitive as a stone . . . philosophy registers . . . facts as valuable psychological material for its investigations." This description suggests the Spirit of the Years. But when the philosopher becomes angry, his "rage turns into a Mephistophelian gallows-humour, that with half-suppressed pity and half-unrestrained mockery looks down with a like sovereign irony both on those caught in the illusion of happiness and on those dissolved in tearful woe."[31] Perhaps to keep the Spirits of the Years and of the Pities free of complications as representatives of stoic thought and compassion, Hardy created the Spirit Ironic to view the world with this "half-suppressed pity and half-unrestrained mockery."

The Spirit Ironic is an ironist, quick to perceive the incongruous or illogical, and then to ward off the pain of the spectacle by viewing it

---
this article, I too associated the Spirits Ironic and Sinister. See p. 1171.

31. Von Hartmann, III, 118-119.

intellectually and laughing at its absurdity. Where he might pity the Austrians humiliated at Ulm, he wards off the feeling by thinking of General Mack's folly and Napoleon's cleverness, and seeing the "phantasmagoric show" as a comedy. He says, "The Will Itself might smile at this collapse/Of Austria's men-at-arms, so drolly done." (I, IV, v, 76) He is amused at any incongruity. When a "Distant Voice in the Wind" calls upon the Russians to defend "your land, your liberty," the Spirit Ironic says: "Ha! 'Liberty' is quaint, and pleases me,/Sounding from such a soil!" (III, I, i, 329)

In many turns of thought, the Spirit Ironic suggests Shakespeare's Mercutio, jesting on a stage vastly larger than Verona. Mercutio's tendency to nick the bubble of love's pretense and to jest at its sacredness appears in the song the Chorus of Ironic Spirits sings when Napoleon meets Marie Louise: "She'll bring him a baby,/As quickly as maybe,/And that's what he wants her to do,/Hoo-hoo!" The Spirit of the Years rebukes the Ironic Spirits, but they mock even this ancient Spirit, saying, "With holy reverent air/We hymn the nuptials of the Imperial pair." (II, V, vi, 281)

This is sophisticated jesting on the level of high comedy. The Spirit Ironic has the learning and experience of the Spirit of the Years.

Where the Spirit of the Years quotes Latin to reconcile himself with the universe, the Spirit Ironic paraphrases a Chorus of Aeschylus's *Agamemnon* to express skeptical amusement about it:

> As once a Greek asked I would fain ask too,
> Who knows if all the Spectacle be true,
> Or an illusion of the gods (the Will,
> To wit) some hocus-pocus to fulfil?
> (After Scene, P. 524)

The Spirit Ironic is *au courant* in science. He draws metaphors from astronomy, geology, and biology. Semichoruses of Ironic Spirits express a determinism like that of the Spirit of the Years—"That things to be were shaped and set/ Ere mortals and this planet met"—and then tell the story of evolution in song. (I, VI, iii, 118-120)

With all his mockery—indeed, underlying it —the Spirit Ironic insists that the Spirits see things rationally. His intellectual view is established in his only words in the Fore Scene: when the Spirit of the Pities speaks of "this terrestrial tragedy," the Spirit Ironic says, "Nay, comedy." (P. 4) He often uses the word *logic*. The Spirit of the Pities, even while observing the Will, "cannot own the weird phantasma real." The Spirit of the Years says that "Affection ever was illogical." The Spirit Ironic comments aside, like a slightly saddened, aging man of the world, that the "mere juvenile" is too young to "own to such logic." (I, I, vi, 36-37) But as the Spirit of the Pities grows in wisdom and protests the "intolerable antilogy" of the Will, the Spirit Ironic agrees: "Logic's in that." (I, IV, v, 77) The Spirit of the Pities stands on logical ground when he points to the enemy soldiers at Talavera who clasp hands as they drink at the same stream. The Spirit Ironic comments wryly that the Will "cannot be asked to learn logic at this time of day!" (II, IV, v, 245) He insists that the Spirits see things as they are. He sees the drunken English deserters singing bawdy songs in a Spanish cellar as "Quaint poesy, and real romance of war!" (II, III, i, 210) When the Spirit of the Pities becomes hysterical at Waterloo and imagines the bones of the long-dead quaking for horror, the Spirit Ironic jerks him back to the fact: "Turn to the real." (III, VII, viii, 515)

The Spirit Ironic is also a showman, but of course he stages an adroit comedy of manners. Caroline, Princess of Wales, is not invited to the Prince Regent's ball, and his morganatic wife, "the Fitzherbert Fair," is invited in an inferior rank, as a "plain 'Mrs.'" to "sit with common dames." Rumors (apparently inspired by the Spirit of Rumour) reach the "two spouses" that a "fresh favourite rules" the Prince's heart, and the two decide to use spurious cards to enter by "the leetle, sly, chair-door," with, as the Spirit Ironic says, "dames of strange repute, who bear a ticket/For screened admission by the private wicket." An Ironic Chorus sings of "A wife of the body, a wife of the mind,/A wife somewhat frowsy, a wife too refined." Whether the wives carry out their intention is left vague. After the Prince has heard rumors that the King is dead and "provisionally throws a regal air into his countenance," the Spirit Ironic says, "Now for the wives," and causes the Prince to hear their voices. The Spirit so manipulates the voices that the unseen wives seem to pounce upon the Prince, "the PRINCESS pouring reproaches into one ear, and MRS. FITZHERBERT into the other." The comedy goes on until the Spirit of the Years, reproving the Spirit Ironic for mocking "The Mighty Will's firm work," calls it off. (II, VI, vi-vii, 310-318)

Though, in his sophisticated way, the Spirit Ironic shares the intellectual view of the Spirit of the Years, he comes close to being a champion of the Pities in the clash of opinion among the Spirits. He listens to the Spirit of the Pities throughout the drama and mocks him when he yields to sentimentality, but as the Spirit of the Pities grows in assurance and logic, supports him. Late in the drama, he acts as a *source* of Causation with an aim like that of the Spirit of the Pities. When the Spirit Ironic thinks that a "little moral panorama" would do Napoleon no harm, he asks the Spirit of the Pities—like a friendly elder offering aid to a neophyte—"Shall it be, young Compassion?" The Spirit of the Pities is despondent: "What good—if that old Years tells us be true?" (III, VI, iii, 467) But the Spirit Ironic goes ahead and presents the panorama that causes Napoleon to lose confidence and perhaps the battle of Waterloo. The Spirit of the Pities at last wins his debate partly by urging that if the Will were aware It would be merciful. This point is stated most sharply by a Chorus of Ironic Spirits that sings: "Of Its doings if It knew,/What It does It would not do!" (III, VII, viii, 517) In the After Scene, faced with the question of whether the universe has a purpose, the Spirit Ironic says, "For one I cannot answer. But I know/ 'Tis handsome of our Pities so to sing." (P. 524)

In his conversation with Archer, Hardy said that "war is doomed" by "the gradual growth of the introspective faculty in mankind. . . . war will come to an end, not for moral reasons, but because of its absurdity."[32] In *The Dynasts*

32. William Archer, "Real Conversations. Conversation 1.—With Mr. Thomas Hardy," *The Critic*, XXXVIII (April, 1901), 316.

it is the Spirit Ironic who attacks war as absurd, and so speaks for Hardy on this point. The comment of the Spirit on the battle of Waterloo expresses Hardy's disillusioned view:

> Warfare mere,
> Plied by the Managed for the Managers;
> To wit: by frenzied folk who profit nought
> For those who profit all! (III, VII, viii, 515)

Like the Spirit Ironic, the Spirit Sinister calls war a comedy. But the Spirit Ironic's view rests on intellectual perception of absurdity; the Spirit Sinister's on his delight in human suffering and gory spectacles. The Spirit Sinister's comedies are: "my pestilences, fires, famines . . . my Lisbon earth-quake . . . my French Terror, and my St. Domingo burlesque." (I, I, i, 8)

I think it probable that Hardy intended to develop the Spirit Sinister more fully than he did, and even differently. That he did not develop the Spirit as fully as he intended is suggested by some figures. When prose speeches are measured in lines of type and poetry in lines, the Spirit Sinister has in the Fore Scene 7 lines; he has in Part First 38 lines; in Part Second, 32 lines; in Part Third, 19 lines (including 3 lines by the Chorus of Sinister Spirits); and in the After Scene nothing at all to say. Further, of the 38 lines in Part First, 24 occur in Act First, with only 14 in the remaining five Acts. One of this Spirit's lines is: "Ay; begin small, and so lead up to the greater." (I, I, i, 8) The development of the Spirit illustrates the opposite process.

In the first speech of each Spirit in the Fore Scene—even the two-word speech of the Spirit Ironic—Hardy indicated the nature of the Spirit and his role in the drama. The Spirit Sinister's first speech, commenting upon the mechanical processes of the Will, reads: "Good, as before./My little engines, then, will still have play." (Fore Scene, p. 1) The word *engines* must mean "machinations" for evil. Then it would seem that Hardy intended the Spirit Sinister as a channel of Causation to transmit evil impulses from the Will to the human characters.

The Spirit Sinister opens the Napoleonic drama. After the Spirit of the Years speaks a three-line speech to invite the Spirits to watch the play, it opens with the Spirit Sinister's claim that he caused the "comedies" mentioned above. But the Spirit of the Years tells him: "Wait./Thinking thou will'st, thou dost but indicate." Then logically, the Spirit Sinister afterwards can only comment, not cause. In the same scene the Spirit Sinister says that he

THE SPIRITS 73

sought to do evil: he "paean'd" the Will to "unimpel" George III to reply to Napoleon in a friendly way, for friendliness would have "marred the European broil." (I, I, i, 8-11) The Spirit of the Years does not repeat his rebuke, but perhaps he has said enough to block Hardy from using the Spirit Sinister to whisper suggestions of evil to the human characters.

Later in this Act First, the Spirit of the Years calls the Spirit Sinister "Thou Iago of the Incorporeal World." (I, I, vi, 34) This speech suggests that Hardy still intended to develop the Spirit Sinister as an agent of motiveless evil—an Iago.

Having put the Spirit Sinister into the drama as an Iago, Hardy sought to characterize him. He gave the Spirit Sinister at first the character of a somewhat cynical ironist who visits the House of Commons because "There's sure to be something in my line toward, where politicians are gathered together!" (I, I, iii, 17) But becoming more interested in the Spirit Ironic and developing him fully and sympathetically, Hardy transferred the role of pointing out ironies to this Spirit. Then the Spirit Sinister had to represent a more malicious cynicism. He expresses the belief that the principle of evil rules the world, saying that the Spirit of the Years could not prove to him by Doomsday "that there is any right or reason in the Universe." (I, I, vi, 34) Thereafter the Spirit Sinister praises sheer evil. Observing with pleasure the grief of Napoleon's soldiers in Russia when they learn that he has deserted them, the Spirit Sinister remarks: "Good. It is the selfish and unconscionable characters who are so much regretted." (III, I, xi, 358) He praises Napoleon, "Excellent Emperor!" for the conscienceless lie that the Prussian troops arriving at Waterloo are Grouchy's reinforcements for the French. (III, VII, viii, 511)

The character of the Spirit Sinister includes the perverseness in human nature that finds thrills in disasters, hangings, and war—or in quieter life, murder stories. The Spirit Sinister says, "My argument is that War makes rattling good history; but Peace is poor reading. So I back Bonaparte for the reason that he will give pleasure to posterity." (I, II, v, 54) He admires murder as an art. Observing the bloody battle of Albuera, he says: "Now he among us who may wish to be/A skilled practitioner in slaughtery,/Should watch this hour's fruition" in order to learn "How mortals may be freed their fleshly cells." (II, VI, iv, 300)

Like Iago, the Spirit Sinister is a cruel jester. But he does not have Iago's delight in lewd visions; he does not speak a lewd line. This is

THE SPIRITS

not a matter of Hardy's delicacy. It seems that Hardy viewed this aspect of Iago intellectually and transferred it to the Spirit Ironic, who has a number of lines mocking love. The Spirit Sinister does exhibit some coarseness of speech. When Napoleon is to be crowned, the Spirit comments cynically upon the Archbishop's words to "one whose aim is but to win/The golden seats that other b---s have warmed." (I, I, vi, 34)

But the Spirit Sinister does not suggest any evil action to any character. His futile paean to the Will is, of course, from himself as a source. He acts only once as a channel of Causation from the Will, in the scene of Napoleon's wedding. But here his speech tempts no one to evil action; it seems only to broadcast a somber thought, not heard by anyone as words but apparently received by a process of telepathy. The effect is only to cast a pall upon a joyful occasion.

In the cast of characters for each Part, Hardy listed "Choruses of Sinister and Ironic Spirits," but the Chorus of Sinister Spirits does not sing or speak a line in Parts First and Second; it sings three lines in Part Third, and that is all. These three lines offer further evidence of Hardy's fluctuating concept of the Spirit Sinister. In the series of lyrics to lament the coming disaster of Waterloo, the Chorus of Sinister Spirits climaxes the lament with a somber song about the death that awaits the sleeping soldiers. The Spirits sing: "And each soul sighs as he shifts his head/On the loam he's to lease with the other dead/From to-morrow's mist-fall till Time be sped!" (III, VI, viii, 484) I do not see anything sinister—any joy in evil—in these lines.

The Spirit Sinister touches the clash of opinion among the Spirits only in expressing fear that if the Spirit Ironic carries his ironies too far he may wake the Will. (II, IV, v, 245)

The relative prominence of the Spirit Sinister in the Fore Scene[33] and in Act First of Part First suggests that Hardy intended him to play a prominent role, perhaps the role of Satan in some major conflict with the forces of good. But Hardy's monism, expressed through the Spirit of the Years, blocked this intention. The impulses of an amoral Will, even when disastrous in effect, are not evil in intention. Hardy must have meant the Spirit Sinister to manipulate his "little engines," but found nothing for the Spirit to do. Instead of revising to cut out the Spirit Sinister, as perhaps he might have done if he had written all three

---

33. He is much more prominent than the Spirit Ironic, who speaks only two words there.

Parts before he published Part First, Hardy rationalized the passivity of the Spirit, even in Part First. When Napoleon is about to be crowned, the Spirit Sinister might have suggested that Napoleon seize the crown himself, but the Spirit realizes that human actions "puppetry remain" and says, "I may as well hold my tongue as desired." (I, I, vi, 34)

It is possible that Hardy created the Spirit Sinister in order to show him as helpless, and let him fade out of the drama toward the end, to suggest that sheer evil, Satan, is not an effective force in human life. In Hardy's system, the ill-contrivance of unconscious process replaces Satan, and therefore the Spirit Ironic takes over!

But I think that the Spirit Sinister's increasingly uncertain and passive role represents an unfulfilled intention. Most of the Spirits speak in verse most of the time; the Spirit Sinister speaks half his lines in prose: 48 lines of prose and 48 of poetry. Perhaps Hardy wrote half of the Spirit Sinister's lines in prose because he did not think this Spirit had poetry in him; or more likely, I think, Hardy found it difficult to feel and express evil in a lyric mood. Following one of the Spirit Sinister's speeches, a Chorus of the Years says, "We comprehend him not." (I, II, v, 54) Perhaps this Chorus speaks for Hardy on this point.

The Spirit of Rumour is a messenger of the Spirits, a sort of subsidiary channel of Causation. He represents the power of the human mind to pick up ideas without sensory perception; sometimes the ideas are accurate, but sometimes they are distortions. When the population of Wessex has heard that Napoleon has landed, two Phantoms of Rumour "in the garb of country-men" join the fleeing pedestrians and tell them accurately that Napoleon has not landed. The pedestrians are not entirely convinced by these Phantoms, though the Phantoms are right. (I, II, v, 54-56) The Spirit of Rumour, disguised as a "young foreigner," accosts a woman of the streets in Paris, for a while pretends ignorance of events, but finally, saying "Channels have I the common people lack," prophesies that Napoleon will not be able to take England. (I, VI, vii, 128-133) Though this Spirit has preternatural powers, the Spirit of the Years does not always trust him to report accurately; when the Spirit of Rumour asks permission to join the throng at Carlton House and confirm the report that Napoleon and Alexander may open hostilities, the Spirit of the Years prefers to go himself because the Spirit of Rumour does not know much more

THE SPIRITS 79

than the human characters. (II, VI, vii, 320) Sometimes the Spirit spreads falsehoods. The Spirit of the Pities, remembering the sad spectacle of insane old King George, thinks it indecent for the Prince Regent to carouse "With the distempered King/Immured at Windsor, sore distraught or dying." The Spirit Ironic thinks that the gloomy faces in the throng reflect "their having borrowed those diamonds at eleven per cent" rather than "their loyalty to a suffering monarch!" To test the fact, the Spirit Ironic sends the Spirit of Rumour to spread a report that the King is dead—a lie that pleases the Prince. (II, VI, vii, 313-314)

The Spirit of Rumour thus serves as a messenger for the other Spirits. He usually asks permission of the Spirit of the Years before he spreads rumors, as he does before he mingles with the throng at a House of a Lady of Quality to spread the rumor that Napoleon has gone to Milan to be crowned Emperor. The news is accurate, not otherwise available to the assembled group. Since no one knows the Spirit, the people conjecture who he is, that is, attributing the rumor they have heard to a variety of sources. (I, I, v, 29-31) The Spirit of Rumour serves the Spirit Ironic in staging his comedy of the Prince Regent's wives, apparently putting ideas into the women's minds as impulses and later, it seems, invisibly pouring reproaches into the Prince's ears in the tones of the women.[34] (II, VI, vi-vii, 310-318)

The Spirit of Rumour takes little active part in the clash of opinion among the Spirits. On the other hand, his generally accurate knowledge of the future gives weight to his surmise that the debate in Commons may react on events and even on the Will, a point in the proposition that the Spirit of the Pities supports. (I, I, iii, 26)

Choruses of Rumours serve throughout the play to report the action being viewed. For example, they report the battle of Talavera (II, IV, iv, 243-244) and part of the battle of Waterloo. (III, VII, i, 484-486)

The Recording Angels, like the Choruses of Rumours, report action. They have books in which they record events and from which, on command, they chant. They enable Hardy to summarize a good many actions in his complex epic-drama.

The Spirit Sinister refers to the Shade of the Earth as a lady. She calls herself "the ineffectual Shade/Of her the Travailler"—the earth.

---

34. The Spirit of Rumour is not shown in these manipulations, but the Spirit Ironic calls on him to reveal the situation and at one point orders: "Messengers, call them nigh!" It seems to me implied that the Spirits of Rumour manipulate the action here, but invisibly.

THE SPIRITS 81

(Fore Scene, p. 3) She opens the epic-drama, questioning what the Will designs in Its manipulation of her processes. Suffering from these processes and seeing them as pointless, she asks the Spirit of the Years:

> What boots it, Sire,
> To down this dynasty, set that one up,
> Goad panting peoples to the throes thereof,
> Make wither here my fruit, maintain it
>   there (I, I, ii, 15)

—when all her suffering could be avoided by "uncreation"?

In the clash of opinion among the Spirits she is on the side of the Spirit of the Pities. When this Spirit, in the Fore Scene, would like to see the earth produce kindly men instead of tyrants, the Shade of the Earth says that she is "not averse." Though the earth is still "curbed and kinged" by It, she does not think it beyond possibility for the evolutionary process to produce men "who love the true, the excellent,/ And make their daily moves a melody." (P. 3) She agrees with the Spirit of the Pities that it is a flaw in nature for men to feel and yet remain puppets. Her special protest against the Will and Its designs is that Its processes blotch her would-be loveliness and disfigure her. At Borodino she protests that the foul fumes and reeks of the battle pollute her air. She does not speak in the After Scene, but the memory of her statement that she is not averse to a kindlier world adds weight to the Spirit of the Pities' arguments.

If one looks at *The Dynasts* as a philosophic document, the human action is an illustration of a thesis. The thesis is developed in a clash of the opinions held by the Spirits.

The opinions held by the Spirits are propositions concerning the nature of the world. The underlying issue is whether the world-process has meaning, purpose, and goal, or not. The idea that this issue might be the theme of discussion in Hardy's long-planned treatment of the Napoleonic wars and that the discussion might end with the victory of the meaningful and merciful—the Pities—perhaps came to Hardy from his reading of Von Hartmann. Von Hartmann said, "Thus the world-process appears as a *perpetual struggle of the logical with the non-logical,* ending with the conquest of the latter. . . . we believe in a final victory of the ever more radiantly shining reason over the unreason of blind volition."[35]

The Spirit of the Years and the Spirit of the Pities debate the propositions of the drama. To the Spirit of the Pities, the world seems ill-contrived, and he asks why. The Spirit of the

35. Von Hartmann, III, 127.

Years says that the world is what it is; in the sense of planned for a purpose, it is not contrived at all. The Spirit of the Pities dares not hold that life has no meaning or purpose. The Spirit of the Years replies that the only purpose shown by the facts is the creation of intricate patterns. To show what the process is and how it works unconsciously, the Spirit displays the Will. But it is both senseless and unjust, says the Spirit of the Pities, for the Will to develop patterns in which Its mechanically moved creations feel pain. This injustice in the Will kills in man the sense of right. The Spirit of the Years replies that the development of consciousness to feel pain was an accident, not an intention in the Will. Then let the Will feel the pain, says the Spirit of the Pities, for It is responsible. As It is unconscious, the Spirit of the Years says, It cannot be held responsible.

Then the Spirit of the Pities surmises that since all living things are parts of It, their pain may waken It to awareness. He argues, when the ugly horror of Borodino wakes even callous Napoleon, that if men have wakened through the ages, the Force within them may waken. The Will may become conscious and aware of pain.

In debate, the Spirit Ironic accepts the Spirit of the Years' version of the Will as fact, but listens to the Spirit of the Pities. When the Spirit of the Pities is too hopeful, the Spirit Ironic mocks his lack of logic and jeers at the notion that the Will may have moral aim. But when the Spirit of the Pities points out the Will's lack of logic in "making figments feel," the Spirit Ironic agrees. He doubts whether the Will can learn logic, but admits that if It could, It would not behave as It does.

The issue is decided in the closing lines of the After Scene. The decision is a victory for the Spirit of the Pities. This Spirit is not able to demonstrate his contentions as facts, but his logic, as well as his feeling, moves both the stoic Spirit of the Years and the sophisticated Spirit Ironic to question—"I cannot answer," says the Spirit Ironic, and "the question rings," says the Spirit of the Years (P. 524)—whether the Will is necessarily and forever unconscious and unfeeling. These Spirits apparently join the Spirit of the Pities in a stirring hymn of hope. This is as far as demonstrable knowledge and rational deduction can go toward acknowledging that the world may finally have meaning, purpose, and goal, and that Von Hartmann's belief in the final victory of consciousness—"of the ever more radiantly shining reason over the unreason of blind volition"—may be right.

When the Spirits are seen as individualized characters in a drama, the clash of opinion seems much more dramatic than a "gathering of emeritus professors of philosophy"[36] sitting in a box in a theatre.[37] They suffer or stoically refuse to suffer; they become angry and lash out at one another, as the Spirit of the Years lashes out at the Spirit Sinister; the Spirits of the Years and of the Pities struggle for the life of Villeneuve; the Spirit of the Pities tries repeatedly to sway Napoleon and succeeds, in part, when the Spirit Ironic comes to his aid; the Spirit of the Pities becomes hysterical at Waterloo; in argument, the Spirits use every human device, including the *argumentum ad hominem,* to put down the young Spirit of the Pities; the Spirit of the Years yields ground reluctantly. The Spirit of the Pities grows in experience, assurance, and stature.

In the foregoing description of the roles played by Hardy's Spirits, I insist that the Spirits are Hardy's characters, not his voice. When the Spirits act as narrators to describe action,

36. Barker Fairley, "Notes on the Form of The Dynasts," *PMLA*, XXXIV, n. s., XXVII (1919), 401-415; p. 401.

37. Perhaps the clash of opinion would seem more dramatic if set apart like the scene in Hell in Shaw's *Man and Superman.* Instead, it is looped into the human drama. It has to develop as a woof to follow the warp of Napoleon's fortunes. Continuity is blurred because the Spirits perform also as narrators. On the other hand, their arguments are given weight and depth because the human drama illustrates them.

as the Choruses of Rumours and the Recording Angels do, or as showmen to display the Will, as the Spirit of the Years does, or human suffering, as the Spirit of the Pities does, they speak for Hardy to "stage" his closet drama. But when they act as characters, express opinions, and argue with one another, they reflect this or that aspect of Hardy's thought, but no one reflects all of it. Hardy's meaning is the meaning of the whole epic-drama, that is, of the action, the comments upon the action, and the conclusion to which it comes.

CHAPTER THREE

The Will as Mind

"WHAT OF THE IMMANENT WILL AND
ITS DESIGNS?"

LONG BEFORE Hardy developed the Immanent Will and his evolutionary meliorism, he brooded upon the apparently aimless operation of natural law to produce creatures who suffer injustice and pain, and he fancied the remorse of law if it were conscious. On May 9, 1881, he recorded in his journal: "After infinite trying to reconcile a scientific view of life with the emotional and spiritual, so that they may not be interdestructive I come to the following: . . . . The emotions have no place in a world of defect, and it is a cruel injustice that they should have developed in it. If Law itself had consciousness, how the aspect of its creatures would terrify it, fill it with remorse!"[1] This meditation upon "Law" suggests that Hardy, before he read Schopenhauer, did not

1. *The Early Life*, p. 192.

suppose the ultimate principle in nature to be Mind, but did entertain the idea as a fancy.

Schopenhauer's *The World as Will and Idea* was translated into English in 1883, and it seems evident that Hardy read it during the composition of *The Woodlanders*, published in 1887. Dissertations and book-length studies have amply shown the influence of Schopenhauer upon Hardy's thought. It seems beyond question that Schopenhauer influenced Hardy to think now of the philosophers' Thing-in-Itself that he had called "Law" as Will. Schopenhauer's Will is the non-conscious basic force that underlies, is expressed by, and also is all phenomena, living and non-living; it is the force that impels all processes, creates all matter, and is immanent in all its expressions. It thrusts blindly within each of its creations, for consciousness abides within it only in the living creatures it inhabits. Brennecke states the attributes of Schopenhauer's Will echoed in Hardy's thought as follows:

1. The Will is One and Immanent. Therefore there is unity in the world, and the universe must be explained in the terms of Monistic Idealism, as opposed to Monistic Materialism and Transcendental Theism.
2. The Will is Groundless and Autonomous. Therefore the universe is ruled by the immutable laws of necessity, determinism is at the base of ap-

THE WILL AS MIND

parent arbitrariness, and chance is only a form and manifestation of necessity.

3. The Will is Unconscious. Therefore there is absolute superiority of Will over intelligence, and all true psychology must start out from the premise that man is primarily a willing, and not a reasoning being.

4. The Will is Aimless. Therefore Pessimism is the only adequate estimate of life.

5. The Will is Indestructible. Therefore a faint ray of an Ultimate Hope may be discerned.[2]

A great deal in *The Dynasts* might support the opinion expressed by Rutland: "there cannot be any doubt that it was Hardy's reading in Schopenhauer after 1884 which determined the final form of the poem on the Napoleonic wars which he had long been meditating."[3] But to read Hardy's epic-drama with the idea that Schopenhauer determined its *final* form leads to curious interpretations. For example, Brennecke reads a song of a Chorus of Ironic Spirits in this way:

That mundane events may vaguely influence the Prime Energy, and that human consciousness may thus react in some mysterious way upon its Fundamental Cause, is the theme of the song of the Ironic Spirits with which the birth of the Emperor's son is celebrated—

2. Ernest Brennecke, Jr., *Thomas Hardy's Universe: A Study of a Poet's Mind*, London: T. Fisher Unwin, 1924, pp. 31-32.
3. William R. Rutland, *Thomas Hardy: A Study of His Writings and Their Background*, Oxford: Basil Blackwell, 1938, p. 96.

> The Will Itself is slave to him,
> And holds it blissful to obey! . . .
>
> It must be observed that this indefinable idea is expressed by the Ironic Spirits, and that its significance is thus perhaps primarily satirical. The whole question: "Shall blankness be for aye?" is felt by the poet to press upon his mind and heart, but it is finally left unanswered.[4]

The words of the Ironic Chorus may be witty overstatement, but examination of the total role of the Ironic Spirits brings into question whether the thought underlying the song is "perhaps primarily satirical." And of course the question of Hardy's meliorism is "finally left unanswered," if the only acceptable answer is scientific demonstration. But that Hardy was playing with an idle fancy, that he did not intend seriously the conclusion toward which the whole drama moves, seems most unlikely. The possibility, Brennecke continues, "is definitely excluded in the system of Schopenhauer."[5] So it is, but Hardy's thought embraced other possibilities than the ones in this system.

As previously suggested, Hardy's reading of Eduard Von Hartmann's *Philosophy of the Unconscious* shortly before or during the composition of *The Dynasts* both supported views

4. Brennecke, *Thomas Hardy's Universe*, pp. 118-119.
5. *Ibid.*

THE WILL AS MIND

adopted from Schopenhauer and modified them. Like Schopenhauer, Von Hartmann postulated all force and matter to be the "phenomena of *one* substance," the Will.[6] But Von Hartmann, while conceiving the *"one* substance" as Will and frequently calling it so, also conceived it as a psychic force or unconscious Mind, which he called the Unconscious. The activity of this Unconscious is manifest in the creative and impulsive forces of natural processes—for example, gravitation, instinct, and evolution—toward fulfilment of an unmeditated purpose. He said that the "immanent unconscious teleology of an intuitive unconscious intelligence is revealed in natural objects and individuals by means of . . . continual creation or conservation." It is impossible for man's limited consciousness to "apprehend the mode of perception of this intelligence," as "we are only able to indicate it through the contrast to our own form of perception (consciousness), thus only to characterise it by the *negative* predicate of *Unconsciousness.*"[7]

Beyond this concept of the Will as unconscious Mind, Hardy found in Von Hartmann the concept that consciousness, as well as impulses from the Unconscious, may be a ground for action. Decisions to act may arise from re-

6. Von Hartmann, II, 184.   7. *Ibid.*, II, 246.

flection upon sensations and perceptions. Then, as consciousness gains in influence during the processes of evolutionary development, consciousness may come more and more to inform the unreflective Mind and lead It toward meditated action. This conception, radically different from Schopenhauer's, underlies Hardy's meliorism.

The philosophers Schopenhauer and Von Hartmann defined the Will as the Thing-in-Itself that includes, in its phenomena and behavior, all things. Hardy sought to indicate the nature of his Immanent Will by giving It many names. In his Preface he called It "the First or Fundamental Energy" and indicated that he did not think the masculine pronoun proper for It, as "a necessary and logical consequence of the long abandonment by thinkers of the anthropomorphic conception of the same." (P. ix) The Shade of the Earth in the first line of the epic-drama calls It "the Immanent Will," though Blunden remarks that Hardy thought this "not quite the precise term he wanted for his conception."[8] Stage directions call It the "Will" and the "Universal Will."[9] The General Chorus of Intelligences

---

8. Edmund Blunden, *Thomas Hardy*, London: Macmillan and Co., 1942, p. 235.

9. To avoid clutter in these lists, I am omitting references to act, scene, and page. Various Spirits call the Will by the same

THE WILL AS MIND

that concludes the Fore Scene calls It "The PRIME . . ./Whose Brain perchance is Space, whose Thought its laws." The Chorus that concludes Part First calls It "That . . . by Whose stress we emanate."

The Spirit of the Years (including, of course, Choruses of the Years) calls it "The Byss," "the Prime Mover of the Gear," "the Willwebs," "the Mode," "the Prime Volitions," "the Cause," "the lobule of a Brain," "A Brain whose whole connotes the Everywhere," "the One," "the Immanent," "the High Influence," "the Cause of things," "this all-inhering Power," "the Great Unshaken," "That/Which was before," "immense unweeting Mind," "a Clairvoyancy," "Chance, in your more humble tongue," "That Which all ordains," "the World-Soul," "the Eternal Urger," "The mutative, unmotived, dominant Thing," "the Master-hand," "the Immanent Shaper," "the Immanent Intent," "the unweeting Urger," "the Mighty Will," "the rapt Determinator," "That within it [Napoleon's Grand Army]," "the Back of Things," "the Immanent Unrecking," "the Unknowable," "the Urging Immanence," "the Great Foresightless," "web Enorm," "Im-

---

name, but I am assigning each name to the Spirit who first uses it and omitting repetitions.

manence," "Loveless, Hateless," "the All-mover," and "the All-prover."

The Spirit of the Pities calls It the "viewless, voiceless Turner of the Wheel," "the Absolute," "That scoped above percipience," "Incognizance," "the Unconscious Cause," "That which holds responsibility," "the Mover," "the Reaper," "Great Necessitator," "the Inadvertent Mind," and "the Force informing [men]." When he paeans the Will as he thinks It ought to be, the Spirit of the Pities uses the terms "some Great Heart," "Thee" (a personality, as opposed to "It"), "Great and Good," "the Well-willer," "the kindly Might," "The Alone, through Whom all living live," and "The Alone, in Whom all dying die."

The Spirit Ironic calls It "That/Which, working all," "Creation," "the Wheel which drives the Infinite," and "the dreaming, dark, dumb Thing." The Spirit Sinister calls It "the Unconscious." The Spirit of Rumour calls It "That, whose outcome we all are." The only human being who names the Will is Napoleon, who calls It "The Genius who outshapes my destinies" and the "pitiless Planet of Destiny."

Two points may be noted in these lists. Various terms indicate the Will to be Mind: "the lobule of a Brain," "A Brain whose whole con-

THE WILL AS MIND

notes the Everywhere," "immense unweeting Mind," "a Clairvoyancy," "the Inadvertent Mind," "the Unconscious," and other terms like "the Immanent Intent" that suggest mind. Yet, though some of the terms might imply pantheism or transcendentalism, no term, except those the Spirit of the Pities uses to paean his hopes, implies that the Will is either a personality or an anthropomorphic God.

Besides naming the Will to indicate Its nature, Hardy pictures It. He does not treat It as a symbol, like his Spirits, who are "impersonated abstractions." It is no abstraction standing for something besides Itself. Hardy presents the invisible, non-material, and non-dimensional Will Itself. His effort is like that of the physics teacher who draws the structure of an atom no eye has ever seen. In the drama, the Will is made momentarily visible as if through an effort of the philosophic imagination that strains even the Spirit of the Years. Hardy's Preface invites us to "look through the insistent, and often grotesque, substance at the thing signified." (P. xi)—Then the Will vanishes. But Hardy keeps It before us in the Spirits as Its channels, their comments upon It, and the behavior of the characters.

The Will is displayed six times. It is displayed in the Fore Scene as "one organism [showing] the anatomy of life and movement in all humanity and vitalized matter included in the display." Looking on, the Spirit of the Pities observes Its pulsations: "Strange waves I sight like winds grown visible,/. . . Twining and serpentining round and through./Also retracting threads like gossamers." The Spirit of the Years explains what he sees:

> These are the Prime Volitions,—fibrils, veins,
> Will-tissues, nerves, and pulses of the Cause,
> That heave throughout the Earth's compositure.
> Their sum is like the lobule of a Brain
> Evolving always that it wots not of;
> A Brain whose whole connotes the Everywhere.
> (Pp. 6-7)

The second time the Spirit of the Years displays the Will, It is "the interior of a brain which seems to manifest the volitions of a Universal Will, of whose tissues the personages of the action form portion." (I, I, vi, 36) In a third display, the Spirits see the "Nerves, sinews, trajects, eddies, ducts of It/The Eternal Urger." The "Immanent Will appears . . . as a brain-like network of currents and ejections, twitching, interpenetrating, entangling, and thrusting hither and thither the human forms." (I, VI, iii, 118) In a fourth display, Hardy writes: "like breezes made visible, the films or brain-tissues of the Immanent Will . . . pervade

THE WILL AS MIND 97

all things, ramifying through the whole army, NAPOLEON included, and moving them to Its inexplicable artistries." (III, I, i, 330) In a fifth display, It is shown as "the electric state of mind" that animates both Wellington and his generals and the French officers. It resembles "as a whole the interior of a beating brain lit by phosphorescence." (III, II, ii, 368) In the final display of the Will, It is not directly likened to a brain, but the image is consistent with the idea of a brain: "The web connecting all the apparently separate shapes includes WELLINGTON in its tissue with the rest, and shows him, like them, as acting while discovering his intention to act." (III, VII, vii, 505)

Three of these displays occur in Part First, and three in Part Third. None occurs in Part Second. Perhaps Hardy, in writing Part Second, supposed he had made the Will clear already, but found on reading reviews that he had not, and again presented It in Part Third.[10] Or perhaps the dramatic action most clearly demanded the displays in Parts First and Third. The Spirit of the Years displays the Will on occasions when the Spirit of the Pities protests Its sway, and the clash of opinion among the Spirits is more intense in Parts First and Third

10. Part First was published in 1904, Part Second in 1906, and Part Third in 1908.

than in Part Second. On the other hand, the Spirits speak of the Will ever and again, in all Parts.

In five of the six exhibitions of the Will, Hardy likens It to a Brain, and in the sixth implies a Brain. All the displays imply that the Brain works not as an engine or even as a force, but as a living organism. This Brain is not apparent to the creatures It manipulates. The Spirit of the Years says that It is:

>   unguessed
> Of those It stirs, who (even as ye [the Pities]
>   do) dream
> Their motions free, their orderings supreme;
> Each life apart from each, with power to mete
> Its own day's measures; balanced, self-complete;
> Though they subsist but atoms of the One
> Labouring through all, divisible from none.
>   (Fore Scene, p. 7)

In the sixth display, the Will acts directly from within the brains of men as motor impulse, the meaning of which is then made apparent—*ex post facto*—to consciousness. The Mind is thus a permeating unity, with the qualities of Von Hartmann's Unconscious—often called the "All-One"—which is "the common bond of the world . . . the indivisible metaphysical essence, as whose objective phenomena the only ap-

THE WILL AS MIND 99

parently substantially separated natural individuals are to be regarded."[11]

Since the attributes of the Will explain the world It expresses and controls, the Spirits discuss these attributes constantly. A fundamental attribute of the Will is a quality of Mind— Its unconsciousness. As the Spirit of the Pities understands it, Its thought is "An automatic sense/Unweeting why or whence," like the reflex actions of which Hardy had read in Von Hartmann and Haeckel. Its thought, says the Spirit of the Years, is a "pulsion" which does not ponder—"weighing not Its thought"—but which thinks on and on in operation of "clocklike laws." (Fore Scene, p. 1) Its thought is continuous; It is an "unrelaxing Will." (I, I, ii, 15) Entranced, "It works unwittingly,/As one possessed." (III, VII, viii, 517) Its thought is within Itself—the universe—which It cannot see from outside; the Spirit of the Years calls It an "in-brooding Will." (I, V, iv, 100) Perhaps a figure of speech from Von Hartmann may underlie Hardy's meaning: like a mirror, It never sees the image It mirrors, for "it lies *behind* it, as the mirror can never mirror itself."[12]

The Spirit of the Pities finds the idea of thinking without awareness difficult to under-

11. Von Hartmann, III, 145.   12. *Ibid.*, II, 227.

stand. He supposes It may be only absent-minded—"Its consciousness/May be estranged, engrossed afar, or sealed" (Fore Scene, p. 2)—and some shock may wake It. But he comes to understand that It is "scoped above percipience." (I, I, vi, 35) The Spirit of the Years offers a careful definition of these strange concepts. He says:

> In that immense unweeting Mind is shown
> One far above forethinking; prócessive,
> Rapt, superconscious; a Clairvoyancy
> That knows not what It knows, yet works
>   therewith. (I, V, iv, 99) [13]

This careful definition was evidently drawn from, and is certainly explained by, a passage in the *Philosophy of the Unconscious*. Von Hartmann says of the Unconscious:

this unconscious intelligence is anything but blind, rather far-seeing, nay, even clairvoyant, although this seeing can never be aware of its own vision, but only of the world, and without the mirrors of the individual consciousnesses can also not see the seeing eye. Of this unconscious clairvoyant intelligence we have come to perceive that in its infallible purposive activity, embracing out of time all means and ends in one, and

---

13. In Hardy's first version, the word *prócessive* was *purposive*. *Rapt, superconscious* was *Yet superconscious*. (American edition, p. 166.) Apparently Hardy revised to express his meaning with precision. *Prócessive* carries the idea of forward-moving sequence, but not of conscious intention, and *Rapt* limits *superconscious*, a word Hardy took from Von Hartmann and did not want misunderstood as "highly conscious."

THE WILL AS MIND

always including all necessary data within its ken, it infinitely transcends the halting, stilted gait of the discursive reflection of consciousness, ever limited to a single point, dependent on sense-perception, memory, and inspirations of the Unconscious. We shall thus be compelled to designate this intelligence, which is superior to all consciousness, at once unconscious and *super*-conscious.[14]

This unconscious Mind works like a weaver half-asleep. Its thinking (say, Its reverie) produces aimless patterns in phenomena. As Its patterns are without design, Its processes seem to the Ironic Spirits like those of fermentation. Or the Mind is, an Ironic Chorus sings, "Like a potter raptly panning!" (III, VII, viii, 517) But the Spirits Ironic have also seen Its processes as "Creation's prentice artistry," expressing "Tentative dreams from day to day." (I, VI, iii, 119) Since what the Mind weaves is an aspect of Itself, the Spirit of the Years calls It a:

> web Enorm,
> Whose furthest hem and selvage may
>   extend
> . . . .
> . . . onwards into ghastly gulfs of sky,
> Where hideous presences churn through the
>   dark. (After Scene, p. 522)

The determinism of the Mind is that of a dream. One asleep cannot control a dream;

14. Von Hartmann, II, 246-247.

one "watches" it. Yet its course is fixed by the contents of the mind. In this way, the Mind dreams "a fixed foresightless dream." (III, VII, viii, 517)[15] That the dream is fixed by the contents of the Mind explains the paradox of Its aimlessness and yet Its determination of events. It seems "To click-clack off Its pre-adjusted laws," (Fore Scene, p. 4) and so "Rules what may or may not befall!" All events are "Fixed . . . immutably!" (I, II, v, 53) All things were "shaped and set/Ere mortals and this planet met," (I, VI, iii, 118) and the Spirit of the Years tells the Spirit of the Pities that "No sigh of thine can null the Plan Predestinate!" (II, VI, v, 304) Rutland objects to this determinism as inconsistent. He says:

But if the Immanent Will simply exists, and by the process of Its existence causes all phenomena, it is clear that there can be no predetermined phenomena. Hardy cannot have it both ways. Either everything is predetermined; or else everything is caused by the gropings of the Will. . . . for predeterminism involves subjection to time. If the events of the year 1805 were, as we are told, "fixed like all else immutably" before the sun emerged from a spiral nebula, then the

15. Hoxie N. Fairchild suggests that *"The Drama of Kings* and *The Dynasts* share a peculiar idea which might be described as the absent-mindedness or entrancement or self-hypnotizing of God." ("The Immediate Source of *The Dynasts*," *PMLA*, LXVII [March, 1952], 62.) Possibly Hardy got the suggestion for the entrancement of the Mind from Buchanan, but the evidence is not convincing. Hardy's concept seems more deeply grounded in the general concept of the Unconscious.

THE WILL AS MIND 103

unfortunate Will, so far from being free to grope comfortably, is to all eternity bound to follow the syllabus drawn up by Itself in an unspecified past.[16]

But the Mind is not "free to grope" exactly; yet It has no drawn-up syllabus. It has an unconscious content that has fixed Its dream, and the sequences of Its impulses are both fixed by this content and listless of aim. Furthermore, it is the Spirit of the Years who asserts that the Mind "ever will so weave." The Spirit of the Pities believes that, informed by human consciousness, It may waken.

The experience of pain and the judgment that pain is evil are products of consciousness. The dreaming Mind is as raptly intent upon the flow of water as upon human suffering. Hardy suggests this point in a stage direction at the battle of Vimiero: "moans of men and shrieks of horses are heard. Close by the carnage the little Maceira stream continues to trickle unconcernedly to the sea." (II, II, vii, 205) This "rapt Determinator . . ./. . . neither good nor evil knows!" (II, VI, vii, 322) A Chorus of Ironic Spirits asks the question: "Are, then, Love and Light Its aim—/Good Its glory, Bad Its blame?"—and answers it: "Nay." (III, VII, viii, 517-518) Before It may be informed by consciousness, the Mind does not know any

16. Rutland, pp. 349-350.

distinction between good and bad. This fact is consistent with Von Hartmann's statement that "Nature, so far as it is *unconscious, does not know* the distinction of moral and immoral. Yes, Nature is in itself not good or bad, but is ever nothing else but natural, *i. e.*, self-adequate. For the universal natural Will has nothing outside itself . . . thus there can be nothing for it good or bad, but only for an individual will."[17]

The Mind is unjust to individuals, for It knows nothing of man's justice. It seems evil to those who suffer. Commenting on the slow, painful death of Nelson, the Spirit of the Pities says, "But out of tune the Mode and meritless/ That quickens sense in shapes whom thou [Years] hast said/Necessitation sways!" (I, V, iv, 99) To the Spirit of the Pities, suffering for the nearly insane old King George, the behavior of the Mind looks like conscious malice. What he observes:

> Might drive Compassion past her patiency
> To hold that some mean, monstrous ironist
> Had built this mistimed fabric of the Spheres
> . . . .
> . . . and not thy said
> Unmaliced, unimpassioned, nescient Will!
> (II, VI, v, 304)

17. Von Hartmann, I, 267.

THE WILL AS MIND 105

But these are expressions of feeling. The unconscious Mind knows no more of malice than of benevolence.

The Spirit of the Pities, insistent upon justice, charges the Mind with responsibility for pain. In a "thorough-sphered melodic rule," helpless men would "Be cessed no pain, whose burnings would abide/With That Which holds responsibility." The Spirit of the Years replies that it is not fair to blame the Mind for what It does not know:

> Nay, blame not! For what judgment can ye blame?
> . . . .
> Your hasty judgments stay,
> . . . .
> O heap not blame on that in-brooding Will;
> O pause till all things all their days fulfil!
> (I, V, iv, 99-100)

The clause "till all things all their days fulfil" suggests that the Mind, even though unconscious, is working to fulfil a purpose, even though unplanned. The Spirit of the Pities speaks of the Mind as "Tranced in Its purpose to unknowingness." (I, I, ii, 15) The point was apparently of some importance to Hardy. In the first version, Hardy had the Spirit of the Years call the Mind "The purposive, unmotived, dominant Thing."[18] In his revision, Hardy changed the line to "The mutative, unmotived, dominant Thing." (II, II, iii, 191) Perhaps he first used the word *purposive* in a special sense that to his mind did not contradict *unmotived,* and if so, perhaps, considering the common use of the words, he changed it to avoid being misunderstood. Duffin considers Hardy's meaning and says: "Can an action be purposive and yet unmotived? Hardy would say yes—with no motive beyond the immediate doing of the action, no regard for consequences. Then can there be even this limited purpose without consciousness? It is doubtless found, practically, in the lowest forms of animal life."[19] For example, a rose may have purpose without conscious motive in manufacturing its fragrance, and a hen in laying an egg. Perhaps Hardy's *purposive* that is consistent with *unmotived* reflects his reading of Chapter III of the *Philosophy of the Unconscious,* which opens with the following statement: *"Instinct is purposive action without consciousness of the purpose.* No one would call Instinct purposive action accompanied by consciousness of the purpose, where therefore the action is a result of re-

18. American edition, p. 81.
19. Henry Charles Duffin, *Thomas Hardy: A Study of the Wessex Novels, The Poems, and The Dynasts*, Manchester: University Press, 1916; third edition, 1937, p. 281.

THE WILL AS MIND 107

flection."[20] If this surmise is right, Hardy must have thought of the Mind as moving toward an unplanned goal in the way that instinct does.

The Mind is not limited by space or time.[21] Of course Hardy was familiar with the concept that space and time are forms of apprehension, and it is impossible to say what sources may underlie the line sung by a Chorus of the Years: "What are Space and Time? A fancy!" and the conclusion that widely separated events are "Parts of one compacted whole." (III, I, iii, 339) As Rutland points out, Hardy read Spencer's *First Principles,* which asks the identical question: "What are Space and Time?" and proceeds to show that "Space, Time, Matter, and, indeed, any ultimate scientific idea, are all representative of realities that cannot be comprehended."[22] The idea of space and time as subjective forms of perception runs through Schopenhauer's *The World as Will and Idea.* Von Hartmann repeats the concept, discussing it at length in relation to the Unconscious. He says:

The Unconscious is not confined to space, for *it first posits* space (the idea the ideal, the will by realisation

20. Von Hartmann, I, 79.
21. "Modern scientific theory compels us to think of the creator as working outside time and space, which are part of his creation, just as the artist is outside his canvas." Sir James Jeans, *The Mysterious Universe,* New York: The Macmillan Company, 1931, p. 155.
22. Rutland, p. 57.

of the idea the real). The Unconscious is thus neither great nor small, neither here nor there, neither in the finite nor in the infinite, neither in the figure nor in the point, neither anywhere nor nowhere. Hence it follows that the Unconscious can have no difference of a spatial nature in it, save so far as it posits the same in imaging and acting. We are accordingly not permitted to say: that which acts in an atom of Sirius *is* something else than that which acts in an atom of the earth, but only: *it acts in a different manner,* namely, locally different.[23]

From such reasoning, Hardy's General Chorus of Intelligences might conclude that the "Brain perchance is Space . . . Thought its laws." (Fore Scene, p. 7) This concept that the Mind lies, so to speak, outside space moves the Chorus Ironic to mock the Spirit of the Pities' attempt to pray to the bodiless, formless "Wheel which drives the Infinite." (II, VI, v, 306)

The Mind is outside time also, in an eternal now. In the *Philosophy of the Unconscious,* Hardy read that "the unconscious representation filling the will is only a non-temporal content, merely dragged along with it, as it were, into time. *Volition* and *activity* are accordingly identical or reciprocal notions. Only through them is Time posited; only through them is the idea hurled from *potential* into *actual* being, from being in the essence into

---

23. Von Hartmann, II, 229.

being in the phenomenon, and therewith into time."[24] It may not matter how Hardy understood Von Hartmann on this point. Apparently Hardy thought of the future held in the Mind as something like the future on a moving-picture film: it is there whether or not it is being projected, and likewise the Brain holds what It holds, whether or not It is conscious.

The Will, Hardy states in his Preface, is a "Fundamental Energy"; It is not merely a *life*-force. Doubtless Hardy had some acquaintance with various vitalist theories, say, those of Lamarck or of Samuel Butler. But even after he had written *The Dynasts,* when he read Bergson's *Creative Evolution*, he rejected the theory of a life-force. In a letter to Dr. Caleb Saleeby, dated March 16, 1915, Hardy said: "An *élan vital*—by which I understand him [Bergson] to mean a sort of additional and spiritual force, beyond the merely unconscious push of life—the 'will' of other philosophers that propels growth and development—seems much less probable than single and simple determinism, or what he calls mechanism, because it is more complex. . . . His partly mechanistic and partly creative theory seems to me clumsy and confused."[25] The Will of *The Dynasts* is "the 'will' of other philosophers," and even if this

24. *Ibid.,* II, 61.   25. *The Later Years,* p. 272.

Will is something more than "single and simple determinism," and more than Hardy cared to define in a letter, Hardy treated It as "the merely unconscious push of life"—and of all other processes.

Both the Intelligences above the human action and Hardy writing the stage directions view men and ripples of water, dictators and snowflakes, as equally significant manifestations of the same Being. This attitude is apparent in Hardy's fiction, for instance, in *The Return of the Native;* it is fundamental in Schopenhauer's concept of the Will and in Von Hartmann's concept of the Unconscious. Hardy found scientific support for the identification of life and non-life in Haeckel's *The Riddle of the Universe,* which says: "The irresistible passion that draws Edward to the sympathetic Ottilia, or Paris to Helen, and leaps over all bounds of reason and morality, is the same powerful 'unconscious' attractive force . . . which unites two atoms of hydrogen to one of oxygen for the formation of a molecule of water. . . . On those phenomena we base our conviction that even the *atom* is not without a rudimentary form of sensation and will . . .—that is, a universal 'soul' of the simplest character."[26]

26. Ernst Haeckel, *The Riddle of the Universe at the Close of the Nineteenth Century* (translated by Joseph McCabe). London: Watts and Co., 1900; edition of 1901, pp. 228-229.

THE WILL AS MIND

In the Dumb Show describing the battle of Leipzig, Hardy compares the soldiers to "conscious atoms": "So massive is the contest that we soon fail to individualize the combatants as beings, and can only observe them as amorphous drifts, clouds, and waves of conscious atoms, surging and rolling together." (III, III, ii, 383) In the Spirit of the Years' first exhibition of the Will, men and "vitalized matter" are presented in parallel phrases: "A new and penetrating light descends on the spectacle, enduing men and things with a seeming transparency, and exhibiting as one organism the anatomy of life and movement in all humanity and vitalized matter included in the display." More typically, Hardy compares human beings to insects. On the map of Europe, presented as a "prone and emaciated figure," the peoples are "seen writhing, crawling, heaving, and vibrating in their various cities and nationalities." (Fore Scene, p. 6) A Recording Angel sings of a vast Austrian army as "molluscs on a leaf," and the stage direction speaks of "The silent insect-creep of the Austrian columns." (I, III, ii, 62) The "huge procession" of Maria Louisa from Vienna to France "looks no more than a file of ants crawling along a strip of garden-matting." The procession is later called "animated dots." (II, V, v, 278) Englishmen building the defenses of Torès Védras "are busying themselves like cheese-mites all along the northernmost frontage." Three "reddish-grey streams of marching men" enter the lines, and "Looked down upon, their motion seems peristaltic and vermicular, like that of three caterpillars." (II, VI, i, 290) Napoleon's Grand Army retreating in the snow from Moscow is a "caterpillar shape," from which men drop off, "are speedily flaked over, and remain as white pimples by the wayside." (III, I, ix, 354) Armies advancing on Waterloo are "crawling hitherward in serpentine lines, like slowworms through grass." (III, VI, i, 454) On the field of Waterloo, English soldiers "hurry to and fro like ants in an ant-hill." (III, VII, i, 484) The Spirit of the Years flays Napoleon and all dictators as "meanest insects on obscurest leaves." (III, VII, ix, 521)

Vice versa, non-life is described in terms of life. A heath in Wessex has "pits like the eye-sockets of a skull." (I, II, v, 53) Before the battle of Ulm, the Danube, "which is swollen by the rainfall and rasped by the storm, seems wanly to sympathize." (I, IV, iv, 74) The barge on which Napoleon meets Alexander "acquires from the current a rhythmical movement, as if it were breathing, and the breeze now and then produces a shiver on the face of

THE WILL AS MIND

the stream." (II, I, vii, 167) The transport ships taking English troops to Spain are "mothlike" and float "like preened duck-feathers across a pond." (II, II, v, 197-198)

These items are metaphors, natural to the point of view of the Spirits above the action. But they also suggest the concept that to the Will men and things rank alike. This concept is expressed. The Spirit of the Years speaks of Napoleon as "Moved like a figure on a lantern-slide," and his Chorus broadens the image to include the army:

> Within the Great Unshaken
> These painted shapes awaken
> A lesser thrill than doth the gentle lave
> Of yonder bank by Danube's wandering wave.
> (I, IV, v, 76-77)

When the Spirit of the Pities laments the English dying in the Scheldt, the Spirit of the Years, speaking of their unimportance to the "Immanent Shaper," says that their cries are like

> the mewling music on the strings
> Of yonder ship-masts by the unweeting wind,
> Or the frail tune upon this withering sedge
> That holds its papery blades against the gale.
> (II, IV, viii, 252-253)

Items of structure suggest man's unimportance to the Will. Napoleon makes a boastful speech to his Grand Army starting for Russia;

the Spirit of the Years exhibits the Will; the figure of Napoleon is "diminished to the aspect of a doll," and shortly "the scene is blotted out by the torrents of rain." (III, I, i, 329-331) Armies marching to cross the Rhine "glide on as if by gravitation, in fluid figures, dictated by the conformation of the country, like water from a burst reservoir; mostly snake-shaped, but occasionally with batrachian and saurian outlines. . . . the winter landscape wears an impassive look, as if nothing were happening." (III, IV, i, 398) Men seem moved by a Mind as raptly intent upon gravity as upon vitality.

This philosophic attitude may, in part, along with Hardy's temperament, underlie the beautiful songs of the Spirit Choruses expressing pity for the dumb creatures of the earth and even the growing grain that "will never be gold," just before Waterloo. (III, VI, viii, 483)

The Will manipulates all phenomena, and in manipulating men moulds history. The Spirit of the Years says of It:

> So the Will heaves through Space, and moulds
>   the times,
> With mortals for Its fingers! We shall see
> Again men's passions, virtues, visions, crimes,
> Obey resistlessly. (II, II, iii, 191)

Napoleon wonders why he takes his army into Russia in spite of portents, has a sudden sense

THE WILL AS MIND

of the Force that "moves me on," and says, "By laws imposed on me inexorably!/History makes use of me to weave her web." (III, I, i, 330)

Though Napoleon feels himself moved by the Will, most men are not aware that It moves them. The Spirit of the Pities points out that men debate in the House of Commons, though "each decision work[s] unconsciously,/And would be operant though unloosened were/A single lip!" (I, I, iii, 26) Men driven to frenzy are especially possessed by impulses of the Will. The Spirit of the Years observes that "all wide sight and self-command/Desert" Napoleon's Old Guard in their suicidal stand at Waterloo, for they are "driven to demonry/By the Immanent Unrecking." (III, VII, viii, 517) Men under Its sway are "mindless minions of the spell," who move "In mechanized enchantment." (III, I, v, 344)

Apparently Hardy visualized the impulses of the Will as something like electric currents. Von Hartmann said of the human will that muscular contraction "takes place through the influence of the motor nerves, by a nerve-current flowing from centre to periphery, a current which is evidently related to the electrical and chemical streams."[27] Hardy visualized the Will as a Brain, with nerves in "innumerable coils."

27. Von Hartmann, I, 169.

(Fore Scene, p. 7) He described Its "brain-like network of currents." (I, VI, iii, 118) In the fifth display of the Will, the action of the Will within the human brain is shown as an "electric state of mind that animates" the officers of the opposing armies. (III, II, ii, 368) Then Its impulses flow through Its nerves as human volitions do, in currents at least "related to" electricity.

That Its impulses seem to spring from the human brain itself echoes Von Hartmann's statement that *"immediate knowledge"* arises in the mind *"as the filling of consciousness with a content (feeling, thought, desire) through involuntary emergence of the same from the Unconscious."*[28]

Chapter Two discusses the Spirits as channels of Causation. The Will pulses without them, but at selected points in the play they dramatize the transmission of impulses by speaking to human beings. The examination of a scene may be useful in illustrating the process. In the scene of Napoleon's marriage to Marie Louise, the Spirits are gathered at the Louvre to attend the wedding. The opening speech, by the Spirit Sinister, strikes the keynote of the scene. Before Napoleon arrives, this Spirit says: "It may be seasonable to muse on the

28. *Ibid.,* I, 363.

THE WILL AS MIND 117

sixteenth Louis and the bride's great-aunt, as the nearing procession is, I see, appositely crossing the track of the tumbril which was the last coach of that respected lady. . . . It is now passing over the site of the scaffold on which she lost her head." The wedding procession enters. The Spirit of the Pities comments that "Napoleon looks content—nay, shines with joy." Then the Spirit of the Years says, "Yet see it pass, as by a conjuror's wand." The stage direction reads: "Thereupon Napoleon's face blackens as if the shadow of a winter night had fallen upon it. Resentful and threatening, he stops the procession and looks up and down the benches." The scene proceeds:

SPIRIT SINISTER
This is sound artistry of the Immanent Will:
it relieves the monotony of so much good-
humour.

NAPOLEON (to the Chapel-master)
Where are the Cardinals? And why not here?
(He speaks so loud that he is heard through-
out the gallery.)

ABBÉ DE PRADT (trembling)
Many are present here, your Majesty;
But some are feebled by infirmities
Too common to their age, and cannot come.

NAPOLEON

Tell me no nonsense! Half absent themselves
Because they *will* not come. The factious fools!
Well, be it so. But they shall flinch for it!

MARIE LOUISE looks frightened. The procession moves on.

SPIRIT OF THE PITIES

I seem to see the thin and headless ghost
Of the yet earlier Austrian, here, too, queen,
Walking beside the bride, with frail attempts
To pluck her by the arm!

SPIRIT OF THE YEARS

Nay, think not so.
No trump unseals earth's sepulchres to-day.
. . . .
. . . No: what thou seest
Springs of thy quavering fancy, stirred to
   dreams
By yon tart phantom's phrase.

MARIE LOUISE (sadly to Napoleon)

I know not why,
I love not this day's doings half so well
As our quaint meeting-time at Compiégne.
A clammy air creeps round me, as from vaults
Peopled with looming spectres, chilling me
And angering you withal!

NAPOLEON

O, it is nought
To trouble you: merely, my cherished one,
Those devils of Italian Cardinals!—
Now I'll be bright as ever—you must, too.

THE WILL AS MIND 119

The ceremony proceeds, with the significant stage direction at its close: "But Napoleon's face has not lost the sombre expression which settled on it." (II, V, viii, 286-289)

Three interpretations are possible. One may think of the Spirits as purely symbolic figures, something like incidental music intended to build a mood in the reader. In this realistic interpretation, some memory of Marie Antoinette rises from the depths of Napoleon's subconscious as he crosses the track of her tumbril and changes his mood. His behavior frightens Marie Louise and changes her mood. Her speeches would indicate that a vivid intuition of Marie Antoinette enters her mind. But in this interpretation the memory is so dim, so buried in the subconscious, that Napoleon is not aware of it except as a feeling. Furthermore, his mood does not change as he crosses the track of the tumbril; it changes after he is in the building among the spectators. The realistic interpretation does not seem to me Hardy's meaning. A second interpretation may consider the Spirits channels of Causation. The Spirit Sinister's opening speech then transmits a fact from the Mind that has bearing upon the wedding, and this fact reaches Napoleon as he comes near the Spirit Sinister. Then the thought is transmitted even more clearly to

Marie Louise, as an image of death. The Spirit Sinister's speech that Napoleon's mood is "sound artistry of the Immanent Will" supports this interpretation. A third interpretation might be that a memory of Marie Antoinette is suggested to the minds of the human spectators when the procession crosses the track of the tumbril. As the Spirit Sinister's words suggest, they "muse on" this memory. The psychic phenomenon called telepathy conveys the memory, as a feeling, to Napoleon when he approaches, and soon thereafter—when she is attuned by fright—to Marie Louise. Perhaps neither thinks definitely of Marie Antoinette; they receive the thought as an apprehension. The Spirit of the Pities (ever sensitive to human feelings) receives clearly the image that Marie Louise receives dimly. The Spirit of the Years receives only what Napoleon receives —an apprehension, without the image of the ghost. In this interpretation, the Spirits do not affect the minds of the human characters and serve only to suggest to the reader the memory that underlies Napoleon's moods. To rationalize all the phenomena of the scene would seem to require an interpretation that combines the last two: the fact is in the Mind; the memory perhaps reaches the spectators through the Spirit Sinister as a channel, before

Napoleon enters; and it is transmitted from the spectators to Napoleon as he comes near them. Then, to some extent, the scene exhibits the psychic phenomenon called telepathy.

The qualities and behavior of Hardy's Immanent Will that is displayed as a Brain and is frequently called the Mind suggest that we may think of It in terms of a philosophic concept that has gained currency since Hardy wrote *The Dynasts,* namely, a Cosmic Mind,[29] and that we may seek to comprehend the evidently psychic phenomena of the epic-drama in the field of investigation that parapsychology is now exploring.

We might first consider the possibility that Hardy had no clear or consistent intention in his portrayal of the Will and the Spirits. His Preface says that the Spirits, at least, "are advanced with little eye to a systematized philosophy." This may mean only that he was not prepared to defend them as representations of fact. It might mean that he was using them chiefly to create effects, say, as Ainsworth used stalking spectres and headless horsemen. Many a criticism of the poem has assumed just this point. Hardy knew some of the older English

---

29. For a brief discussion of this concept, see William Pepperell Montague, "Does the Universe Have a Mind?" *The Saturday Review of Literature,* XXX (September 6, 1947), 9-10 and 31-32.

dramas, and one finds a basis for believing even, as one critic does, that Hardy was imitating medieval religious plays unsuccessfully.[30] Not only had Hardy read Ainsworth's frankly Gothic novels and Dickens's novels that use ghostly materials to suggest psychic apprehensions,[31] but he had written novels with similar suggestions of the supernatural in them.

Ruth Firor says that Hardy used such devices as premonitions to "enhance the mysterious splendor of *The Dynasts*. The atmosphere of the drama is murky, like the air before a thun-

---

30. The struggle of the Spirit of the Pities and the Spirit of the Years to influence Villeneuve has some of the aspects of a morality play. See C. E. Whitmore, "Mr. Hardy's *Dynasts* as Tragic Drama," *MLN*, XXXIX (1924), 455-460.

31. For example, in Chapter XLVI of *Oliver Twist*, as Nancy is on the point of revealing information about Monks, she has a strong premonition of her death: "'I don't know why it is,' said the girl, shuddering, 'but I have such a fear and dread upon me to-night that I can hardly stand.'

"'A fear of what?' asked the gentleman, who seemed to pity her.

"'I scarcely know of what,' replied the girl. 'I wish I did. Horrible thoughts of death, and shrouds with blood upon them, and a fear that has made me burn as if I was on fire, have been upon me all day. I was reading a book to-night, to wile the time away, and the same things came into the print.'

"'Imagination,' said the gentleman, soothing her.

"'No imagination,' replied the girl in a hoarse voice. 'I'll swear I saw "coffin" written in every page of the book in large black letters,—aye, and they carried one close to me, in the streets to-night.'

"'There is nothing unusual in that,' said the gentleman. 'They have passed me often.'

"'*Real ones*,' rejoined the girl. 'This was not.'"
Charles Dickens, *Oliver Twist*, The Authentic Edition, London: Chapman and Hall, and New York: Scribner's, 1901, III, 291.

THE WILL AS MIND

derstorm; the sky is full of half-hidden light that threatens any moment to blaze forth in terrible glory."[32] Brennecke, though taking Hardy's use of Schopenhauer seriously, compares Hardy's use of psychic phenomena in the play with that of Aeschylus. He says, "Both poets display a temperament taking a keen and naive delight in playing with all the old machinery and tinsel belonging to the realm of the ghost-story. Dramatic use of prophecies, premonitions, ominous happenings, and similar astrological 'business' is not disdained by either."[33] No doubt Hardy did intend to enhance the splendor of his drama, and he was temperamentally fond of the old machinery. His notations during the years he was pondering *The Dynasts* include schemes for the use of the supernatural, like that of 1887 for "Napoleon . . . haunted by an Evil Genius or Familiar" and for the use of necromancy to enable Napoleon "to see the thoughts of opposing generals."[34]

But between these notations and the composition of the drama, Hardy discussed psychic phenomena with various people, and he read

32. Ruth A. Firor, *Folkways in Thomas Hardy*, Philadelphia: University of Pennsylvania Press, 1931, p. 34.
33. Ernest Brennecke, Jr., *The Life of Thomas Hardy*, New York: Greenberg, 1925, pp. 248-249.
34. *The Early Life*, p. 266.

the *Philosophy of the Unconscious.* In his conversation with Archer, discussed in Chapter One, Hardy mentioned Von Hartmann in connection with psychic phenomena and admitted that something like telepathy is "conceivable— that there is nothing in it which contradicts the very laws of thought." He did not state belief in psychic phenomena; he demanded evidence. But he went far enough toward belief to warrant his serious use of these phenomena in his epic-drama and the hope expressed in his Preface that the Spirits "may have dramatic plausibility." The sober tone in which Hardy discusses their plausibility within a monistic theory of the universe would seem to rule out his use of the Spirits for Gothic effects alone.

The point—the only point for which I contend—is that the phenomena of *The Dynasts,* though used with some eye to the old effects of Gothic fiction, are psychic phenomena rationally developed, or at least rationalized, within a concept of Cosmic Mind.

It may be difficult to see the difference between the materials of superstition and psychic phenomena. Both deal with experiences, imaginary or real, beyond the present ability of science to explain, fully reproduce, and demonstrate. The line between them lies in the attitude of the observer. Superstition

THE WILL AS MIND 125

rests upon an unreasoning, fearful attitude toward the unknown. The materials of superstition are sheeted ghosts, witches, werewolves, demons, and devils; the laws of superstition are luck, magic, abracadabras, and necromantic rituals—laws of caprice rather than rationally related cause and effect. Superstition demands no rational theory of the universe and of natural law.

The attitude of students of psychic phenomena, on the other hand, is that these phenomena are governed by natural laws that differ from those of chemistry and physics only in not being understood as yet. These men call psychic phenomena manifestations of "extrasensory perception," and they call their science "parapsychology."[35] They have classified the

35. The methods and controls of parapsychology include classifying instances, conducting experiments, tabulating results, and studying them with caution, skepticism, and logic. This science, not yet admitted by all psychologists to be fruitful, is none the less supported by responsible foundations and universities, for example, in the Parapsychology Laboratory headed by Dr. J. B. Rhine of Duke University. Its subject matter of extrasensory perception is technically known as *esp*. This term is defined in *The Journal of Parapsychology* (Duke University Press, Durham, N. C.) as: "Response to an external event not presented to any known sense." ("Glossary," XVII [June, 1953], 159.) Psychic phenomena in general are called *psi*, defined as: "A general term to identify personal factors or processes in nature which transcend accepted laws. It approximates the popular use of the word 'psychic' and the technical one, 'parapsychical.'" (*Ibid.*, p. 159.) Psi "can manifest itself in a variety of ways—as telepathy . . . as clairvoyance . . . and as precognition, or foreknowledge . . . of future events." (Aldous Huxley,

phenomena under such technical terms as *telepathy, clairvoyance, precognition,* and *psychokinesis.* These scientists report that the phenomena seem to be impulses in the subconscious mind,[36] from which they emerge into

---

"A Case for ESP, PK and PSI," *Life*, XXXVI [January 11, 1954], 97.) In order for an occurrence to be technically classified as psychic, "First, the event has to be attributable to some sort of personal agency or causation. It is more than an impersonal happening like a flash of lightning; some personality must be involved. Second, there must be no reasonable explanation as to how the event could have been produced, no explanation, that is, in terms of the orthodox science of today. A psychic experience, then, is a kind of miracle—that is to say, an inexplicable phenomenon—but not attributed to divinity." (J. B. Rhine, *New World of the Mind*, New York: William Sloane, 1953, p. 5).

36. "The discovery that psi functions at an unconscious level advanced the rational understanding of psi more than any other psychological observation that has been made about it." (Rhine, p. 83.) Yet the impulse, not differentiated by the mind from any other impulse, reaches "across the frontier into consciousness by utilizing one of the conscious devices or mechanisms or functions. If the subject is awake, the barest essential meaning may filter through, either partially or completely, without elaboration. It is just a simple impulse: 'I must go home'; or an elemental fear: 'Something terrible has happened'; or a telegraphically brief thought: 'Dan won't be back.' This type of experience is familiar as *intuition.* Or, again, perhaps depending upon the personality of the individual, there will be a more vivid, dramatic experience and the percipient. . . . will see an apparition that symbolizes the significant fact or meaning, or he will hear a voice warning him." (Rhine, pp. 109-110.) Warnings seem not to be precognitions of what *must* be, but of what *may* be if the warning is not heeded. Rhine gives numerous examples, for instance, the authenticated story of a woman who waked in a hotel room at 2:00 a.m. with an urgent impulse to go home at once; she aroused her sleepy husband and persuaded him to get up and drive home through the night. Shortly after she left the hotel, a disastrous fire broke out there. (Rhine, p. 18.)

THE WILL AS MIND

consciousness, and that all seem to be slightly different manifestations of the same force.[37] In some speculations, the phenomena studied in parapsychology are related to the philosophic concept of a Cosmic Mind.[38]

A frequent sense of haunting in *The Dynasts* seems to spring from Hardy's somewhat similar theory of the Mind. There is a sense of haunting on the field of Austerlitz: "The invisible presence of the countless thousands of massed humanity that compose the two armies makes itself felt indefinably." (I, VI i, 109) There is a sense of haunting as the Spirits whisper to

---

37. The divisions "probably should be thought of as just chalk lines that have been drawn on the surface for convenience of usage." (Rhine, p. 91.) It is assumed that some fundamental energy underlies all psychic phenomena: "Back of psi, then, and of all the rest of nature must be some sort of common energetic reality." (Rhine, p. 163.) Psychic phenomena "are necessarily energetic in character even though no energy described in the physics textbooks of today be involved. The suggestion is that in psi processes some form of energy is active that is peculiarly psychological." (Rhine, pp. 199-200.)

38. The relationship is summed up by Aldous Huxley: "There is as yet no satisfactory philosophical theory about psi. Perhaps William James was on the right track when he suggested that we live immersed, so to speak, in 'a continuum of cosmic consciousness,' a World Mind, a little of which filters into every particular brain and is experienced by the owner of that brain as his private mind or consciousness. Henri Bergson went a little further. Mind in itself, he said, is aware of everything, everywhere, without regard to space or time, but the function of our brains is to shut out most of this (to us, irrelevant) knowledge, just in the interests of biological efficiency. On this hypothesis, psi would represent a leakage into personal consciousness of some of the mental material which the brain either normally excludes or directs into utilitarian channels." (Huxley, p. 102.)

Napoleon at a crisis, when he enters Russia or in the wood after Waterloo. But he does not see them as ghosts; their words seem to sound within his brain. These effects seem to be those of psychic phenomena. The phenomena are more serious, more in line with the studies of the Society for Psychical Research—which Hardy mentioned in talking with Archer—than anything in folklore.

One basis for treating these phenomena as manifestations of the Mind was the *Philosophy of the Unconscious*. Von Hartmann discusses incursions of the clairvoyant Unconscious into the human mind, as pulsations that fill consciousness with a content. Its incursions are "independent of the conscious will of the moment, but rather altogether dependent on the interior interest in the object, on the deep needs of the mind and heart for attaining this particular goal." These incursions, says Von Hartmann, explain "clairvoyance in dreams which come true, visions, spontaneous and artificial somnambulism." Flashes of clairvoyance are always concerned with one's self, "important points of one's own future, warning against danger, consolation for sorrow . . . or they make disclosures concerning beloved persons, wife and child, announce *e. g.*, the death of the absent, or imminent misfortune; or, lastly, they

THE WILL AS MIND

relate to events of awful magnitude and extent."[39] That Hardy believed the phenomena he created to be representations of fact cannot be shown. That he worked them out in a fairly consistent pattern and made use of them in preference to ghosts and witches seems a fact.

Hardy did not know the speculations of today's parapsychology, for this science, if still in its infancy, was in its embryo when he wrote *The Dynasts*. Yet the psychic phenomena of the play, developed from Von Hartmann's concepts, resemble the phenomena of extrasensory perception, namely, telepathy,[40] clairvoyance,[41] precognition,[42] and psychokinesis.[43] The phenomena of *The Dynasts* are seen to be psychic in these forms when we see that the Spirits are (among other things) channels of Causation.

Telepathy in *The Dynasts* is usually repre-

---

39. Von Hartmann, II, 56-57.

40. Defined by parapsychologists as "Extrasensory perception of the mental activities of another person. It does not include the clairvoyant perception of objective events." ("Glossary," p. 160.) It is "mind-to-mind contact over the barriers of space." (Rhine, p. 23.)

41. "Extrasensory perception of objective events as distinguished from telepathic perception of the mental state of another person." ("Glossary," p. 158.)

42. "Cognition of a future event which could not be known through rational inference." ("Glossary," p. 159.)

43. "The direct influence exerted on a physical system by a subject without any known intermediate physical energy or instrumentation" ("Glossary," p. 159) —that is, "the direct action of mind on matter." (Rhine, p. 22.)

sented as words spoken by the Spirits to human beings, transmitting a thought or impulse from the Mind. There are many examples, as in the Spirit of the Years' various communications with Napoleon. But there are suggestions of communication from one human mind to another. In England, after Trafalgar, Pitt is acclaimed the "Saviour of England" and his health is "drunk with acclamations." (I, V, v, 103) When Napoleon at Austerlitz hears of Trafalgar, he thinks of Pitt and feels the distant hostility as a haunting:

> 'Tis all a duel 'twixt this Pitt and me;
> And, more than Russia's host, and Austria's flower,
> I everywhere to-night around me feel
> As from an unseen monster haunting nigh
> His country's hostile breath! (I, VI, i, 112) [44]

The communications of the Spirit of the Years to Villeneuve certainly represent impulses from the Will. But communications from the Spirit of the Pities cannot be from the Will, for they oppose the Will. They may symbolize Villeneuve's awareness of suffering and his compassion, but they may also be surmised as feelings

---

44. In the first version, the word *feel* was *scent*. (American edition, p. 186.) Possibly Hardy made the change, destroying the consistent metaphor "scent . . . breath," to suggest that the perception was not sensuous. Von Hartmann stressed that communications from the Unconscious occur as *"feelings* or *moods."* See, for example, I, 97.

THE WILL AS MIND 131

transmitted to Villeneuve through Pities as a channel of human suffering. At any rate, the Spirit of the Pities' "Better, far better, no percipience here" seems to come "From skies above me and the air around," along with the Spirit of the Years' whisper of permission from the Will for Villeneuve to kill himself. (I, V, vi, 105) Apparently the scene of Napoleon's wedding examined above exhibits telepathy: the thought in the spectators' minds is transmitted to Napoleon as a feeling and then from theirs and his to Marie Louise's mind as an even more vivid apprehension.

Clairvoyance is symbolized in the frequent communications of the Spirit of Rumour with human characters. Observing a ball in the House of a Lady of Quality in London, the Spirit of Rumour asks the Spirit of the Years for permission to join the dancers "and all blandly kindle them/By bringing, ere material transit can, a new surprise!" Dressed as a "personage of fashion," the Spirit enters the scene and tells the throng that Napoleon has left Boulogne and gone to Milan, "there to glory him/In second coronation by the Pope." He mingles with the crowd, who suppose him to be Norton, or Stewart, or Lord Abercorn, or "some lively buck,/Who chose to put himself in masquerade." He disappears, but a Lady has an eerie feeling: "Something uncanny's in it all, if true./Good Lord, the thought gives me a sudden sweat,/That fairly makes my linen stick to me!" (I, I, v, 29-31) The scene is paralleled when the Spirit of Rumour appears on the streets of Paris, gives a woman a good deal of news of distant events, and arouses in her the same eerie feeling: "I like not your queer knowledge, creepy man./There's weirdness in your air." (I, VI, vii, 129-133) In each of these instances, the Spirit of Rumour is sent by the Spirit of the Years, and perhaps to some extent he speaks as a channel of the Mind. But what he transmits is not impulses; it is news of distant events. The scenes must mean that news is perceived and rumored in London and Paris before the news can be known through "material transit." In one place, at least, clairvoyance takes place without the intervention of the Spirits. After Napoleon's son is born, Napoleon asks what news has come from Spain. Berthier replies, "Vaguely-voiced rumours, sire, but nothing more,/Which travel countries quick as earthquake-thrills,/No mortal knowing how." (II, VI, iii, 297)

Precognition, especially of the coming of death, occurs throughout the drama, both when the Spirits act as channels and when they merely observe. Von Hartmann, speaking of "presentiments not merely of one's own death, but also of that of dearly-loved persons with whom we are closely linked," says that these presentiments come from the clairvoyance of the Unconscious, in which all phenomena of past, present, and future are contained. Each presentiment comes into the subconscious mind as an impulse and is then symbolized to consciousness. "Frequently the presentiments in which the clairvoyance of the Unconscious is revealed to consciousness are dark, incomprehensible, and symbolical, because they are obliged to take a sensible form in the brain."[45]

The Spirit of the Years acts as a channel through whom the Mind speaks to Nelson of his coming death. A stage direction says, "The Spirit of the Years whispers to NELSON," and Nelson speaks of "warnings, warnings . . . as 'twere within me." (I, II, i, 39) The Spirit of the Years speaks to Brunswick, telling him that "thou this day shalt feel his [Death's] fendless tap,/And join thy sire!" Brunswick starts up, "stirred by inner words,/As 'twere my father's angel calling me,—/That prelude to our death my lineage know!" (III, VI, ii, 459) It is reported that Brunswick's father had the same warning, though no Spirit is presented as a channel of the Mind. When the elder Bruns-

45. Von Hartmann, I, 108.

wick is killed, Hohenlohe says, "Many a time of late/Has he, by some strange gift of foreknowing,/Declared his fate was hovering in such wise!" (II, I, iv, 159) As Von Hartmann suggested, a wife might feel a precognition of her husband's death. Before the battle of Salamanca, Mrs. Prescott says, "This coming battle frightens me!" and the Spirit of the Years, only observing, says that she feels "her prescient pang of widowhood." (III, I, ii, 333-334) She finds her husband dead on the battlefield the next day. Precognition is not limited to foreknowledge of death. Marie Louise parts with Napoleon, saying, "I have an apprehension—unexplained—/That I shall never see you any more!" and the Spirit of the Years explains that she will not see him, though the reasons why—partly her attraction to Count Niepperg—"would pass her own believing" at this time. (III, IV, ii, 401)

The most startling series of precognitions of death are those witnessed by the Spirits as officers leave the Duchess of Richmond's ball for Waterloo. Perhaps Von Hartmann's suggestion that the "clairvoyance of the Unconscious" may appear in "symbolical" form caused Hardy to dramatize the foreknowledge of death as phantoms that dance in front of the departing officers. The Spirits see the phantoms and say that the human beings see them too. The Spirit of the Pities says that Brunswick, who had spoken of his "inner words," "saw and knew" his phantom. The Spirit of the Pities continues:

> One also moved before Sir Thomas Picton,
> Who coolly conned and drily spoke to it;
> Another danced in front of Ponsonby,
> Who failed of heeding his.—De Lancey, Hay, Gordon, and Cameron, and many more
> Were footmanned by like phantoms from the ball.

The Spirit remarks of the human characters that "Some of themselves beheld it; some did not." Ponsonby, it seems, was not psychic, and saw nothing. (III, VI, ii, 462-463)

In cataloging the reported phenomena of psychokinesis, Rhine speaks of it as usually associated with death: "The clock stops, a picture falls, a window shade flies up, or a vase breaks, all in some unexplainable fashion at the time a person connected with the object dies."[46] But the two clear instances of psychokinesis in *The Dynasts* are not connected directly with an individual death. When Maria Louisa tells Metternich that she will marry Napoleon, "A slight noise as of something falling is heard in the room." A portrait of Marie

46. Rhine, p. 34.

Antoinette, standing on a table, has slipped down on its face. The Spirits observe, but apparently do not affect the scene. The Spirit of the Years relates the phenomenon at once to the Will, saying, "What mischief's this? The Will must have Its way." The Spirit Sinister comments that "Perhaps Earth shivered at the lady's say?" and the Shade of the Earth replies, "I own thereto. When France and Austria wed/ My echoes are men's groans, my dews are red." (II, V, iii, 272) The Earth itself, then, by this decision made aware of future events in the Mind, shudders. Again, when Napoleon's son is born dead, the child comes to life when Napoleon enters the room. Whatever the explanation may be in fact,[47] Hardy's explanation is that Napoleon's feeling made the "Will Itself ... slave to him." (II, VI, iii, 298) This effect of Napoleon's strong desire upon the Will, to cause It to alter a fact in the life-process, parallels an item in the larger theme of the epic-drama, the effect of the human mind upon the Cosmic Mind.

The attributes of the Mind discussed in this chapter derive from philosophic interpretation

---

[47]. Historians record that Napoleon's son was apparently born dead. For instance, the Duchess D'Abrantes (Madame Junot), *Memoirs of Napoleon, His Court, and His Family*, New York: 1857, says: "Nearly ten minutes elapsed before he evinced any signs of life." II, 261.

THE WILL AS MIND

of the laws of nature that implement Its thought. It has another attribute or potential, not observed, but surmised on the basis of analogy. If the Mind is unconscious, as if asleep, It may wake. All Its phenomena are parts of It. The consciousness of each conscious part of It lies within It. As more and more of Its parts, that so recently developed consciousness from unconscious process, become conscious, It as a whole may become so. Hardy found support for this idea in the *Philosophy of the Unconscious:*

> We have admitted that it is the Unconscious itself which attains consciousness in the organised individuals. It follows from this that . . . the Unconscious must be regarded as cause of consciousness. It would, however, be very vicious reasoning to try to draw the inference that Consciousness must already inhere in the said Unconscious, else otherwise it could not come out of it. This conclusion would be just as incorrect as the conclusion often, in fact, drawn by savages and the uncultured, that the fire must always lurk *as* fire in the steel and flint, since otherwise it could not leap forth as sparks on their impact. This much only is correct, that there must be contained in the cause the sum of all the indispensable and sufficient conditions in order that the effect may emerge or result from them.[48]

Consciousness does not exist *as* consciousness in Hardy's Mind as a whole, but the "indispens-

48. Von Hartmann, II, 253-254.

able and sufficient conditions" exist in It that existed in each part of It which developed consciousness from unconscious process. Von Hartmann states, indeed, that this development of consciousness, at least in the animal kingdom, is the unconscious purpose of the evolutionary process: "the raising of consciousness presents itself as the purpose of the animal kingdom. Whether one seeks the end of this clearer consciousness in an increase of enjoyment, or of knowledge, or finally of an ethical moment, the elevation of consciousness always remains the direct end of all animal organisation."[49] On this basis, it would seem, Hardy looks forward to the gradual spread of consciousness through more and more living beings, until at last the Mind as a whole becomes conscious. Hardy builds his evolutionary meliorism, examined in Chapter Four, on this surmise that the Mind has the potential of developing consciousness.

All these attributes of the Unconscious do not define It. It is beyond definition. Years says that the full scope of the Will "no mind can mete." (Fore Scene, p. 2) Of the problem why It creates and pulses, he says, "Nay, something hidden urged/The giving matter motion." (I, I, ii, 15) The Chorus Ironic points out Its

49. *Ibid.*, I, 185-186.

THE WILL AS MIND

unimaginable extent, on into the darkness where "ultra-stellar night-webs knit." (II, VI, v, 306) A General Chorus of the Intelligences sings:

> The PRIME, that willed ere wareness was,
> Whose Brain perchance is Space, whose Thought
>   its laws,
> Which we as threads and streams discern,
> We may but muse on, never learn.
>   (Fore Scene, p. 7)

Besides displaying the Will and discussing Its attributes through the words of the Spirits, *The Dynasts* exhibits Its operation in human life in four aspects. (1) In manipulating Its puppets and through them history, It thrusts without purpose. (2) The Will inhabits the characters of the drama as impulses, hungers, and blind energies. (3) The bodies of the characters, when sluggish, unfit, or weary, impede the operations of the Will. And (4) men who are capable of disinterested reason, compassion, and moral courage resist the impulses that come from It.

(1) Since the Will is unconscious, It thrusts toward no meditated goal. The Spirits Ironic believe that, if the evolutionary story indicates progress, the progress is an accident. In the ages before the Spirit of the Pities was born, they observed "Whole nigh-perfected species

slain/By those that scarce could boast a brain."
(I, VI, iii, 119) The action of the Will in recent history exhibits a similar pointless building up of a nation just to knock it down. Such is the story of Poland, knocked down by Prussia, and the story of Prussia, knocked down by Napoleon. "So," says the Spirit Ironic, "the Will plays at flux and reflux still." The Will operates in all sides of every struggle. The Will in Napoleon urges him to crush England, "But," a Chorus of Ironic Spirits sings, "the weaving Will from eternity,/. . . Evolved the fleet of the Englishry." (II, I, vi, 162-165)

(2) The Will operates in human beings as egoistic and selfish impulses. When the Spirit of the Pities pleads with Napoleon to reject the imperial crown, the Spirit speaks for human liberty, the welfare of mankind. Napoleon seizes the crown for his own glory, and this action, says the Spirit of the Years, does "but outshape Its governing." (I, I, vi, 36) Dynasts moved by the Will, a Chorus of the Pities laments, act "Each for himself, his family, his heirs;/For the wan weltering nations who concerns, who cares?" (I, VI, v, 125)

Impulses of the Will, acting as blind energies, move men to rashness in action, even to self-destruction. Villeneuve finally decides, come what may, to obey the Will, represented by

THE WILL AS MIND 141

Napoleon's command. He advances to Trafalgar, and there this meditative, compassionate man suddenly "grows rash, and, darkly brave,/ Leaps to meet war, storm, Nelson—even the grave." (I, V, i, 81) General Mack at Ulm needs all his wits when Napoleon suddenly appears at his "back door." He had soberly decided to keep the body of his troops "here with me." As the officers debate and "gusts call into the chimney, and raindrops spit on the fire," Mack becomes suddenly restless. The Spirit Sinister comments, "The Will throws Mack in agitation:/Ho-ho—what he'll do now!" Mack says, "I have it. This we'll do," and orders his troops dispersed. A General comments that this "seems of all expedients worst" —as it is. (I, IV, iii, 69-73)

Napoleon acts rashly in response to his impulse to marry Marie Louise. The Act in which he makes this decision opens with an effort of the Spirit of the Pities to make Napoleon give up his wars. Countering the Spirit's suggestion, Napoleon asserts his egoistic ambition and thinks of planting his standard in "future time." This obedience to the Will apparently stimulates Its impulses in him, and he decides to throw over the wife "Bespoke . . . from Alexander's house" and marry Marie Louise. He does not pause to think it over, but speaks to Madame Metternich at once. He cannot wait, but demands that she broach the subject to the Ambassador "Now, here, tonight." (II, V, i, 253-257) The result is the debacle in Russia.

Sir Thomas Picton sees his death-phantom grimacing before Waterloo, and moved by the Will, he rushes to meet death. In the battle, he rides conspicuously and, when he is cautioned against his rashness, says, "What the hell care I,—/Is my curst carcase worth a moment's mind?—/Come on!" He "falls dead, a bullet in his forehead." (III, VII, ii, 490) The Will moves cornered men beyond rashness into madness. The battle of Waterloo is virtually over when Colonel Halkett shouts to General Cambronne of Napoleon's Old Guard: "Surrender! And preserve those heroes' lives!" Cambronne replies, "Mer-r-r-rde! . . . You've to deal with desperates, man, to-day!/Life is a byword here!" Then "Hollow laughter, as from people in hell, comes approvingly from the remains of the Old Guard. The English proceed with their massacre." (III, VII, viii, 516-517)

(3) But the Will does not have everything Its own way. When men are sluggish, unfit, or weary, their bodies impede the impulses from the Will. Sluggishness of temperament im-

pedes the Will in the Prussians who face Napoleon on the field of Jena. The Prussians are angry with Napoleon; they are enthusiastic about gallant Queen Louisa, "sent by Heaven to kindle us"; the soul of the nation is "aflame" for war. This result is the doing of the Will; as the Spirit of the Years says, "So doth the Will objectify Itself/In likeness of a sturdy people's wrath." But the streams of the Will flowing in them are impeded. The Spirit of the Years says:

> Uncertainty, by fits, the Will doth work
> In Brunswick's blood, their chief, as in themselves;
> It ramifies in streams that intermit
> And make their movement vague, old-fashioned, slow
> To foil the modern methods counterposed!
> (II, I, iii, 155-156)

The Dynasts presents a detailed study of this impediment to the Will in the gradual weakening of Napoleon's bodily vigor. When Napoleon meets with Alexander of Russia on the River Niemen, "The EMPEROR looks well, but is growing fat." (II, I, vii, 167) Just before Napoleon turns back from Spain, deserters in a cellar observe him. A stage direction says: "The light, crossed by the snow-flakes, flickers on his unhealthy face and stoutening figure."

(II, III, ii, 212) He is in bad physical condition as he watches his Grand Army march into Russia: "It is a day of drowsing heat, and the Emperor draws a deep breath as he shifts his weight from one puffed calf to the other." (III, I, i, 329) Ill-health impedes his genius at Borodino. Before the battle, there is "A coughing heard in NAPOLEON's tent." An aide says it is "The Emperor's. He is thus the livelong day." Napoleon's voice within the tent speaks in "husky accents." During the battle, "The Emperor walks about, looks through his glass, . . . and drinks glasses of spirits and hot water to relieve his still violent cold, as may be discovered from his red eyes, raw nose, rheumatic manner when he moves, and thick voice in giving orders." He says that this battle is "the sun of Austerlitz!" "NAPOLEON sips his grog hopefully." But the Spirit of the Pities remarks that something has happened to Napoleon's usually single-minded concentration on victory; an emotion alien to the thrust of the Will moves him to think of the "vain uncouthness" of the battle. The Spirit of Rumour reports that "Murat cries/. . . Napoleon's genius flags inoperative." The battle "dies resultlessly away"—no Austerlitz! (III, I, iv-v, 340-344) Napoleon's officers comment upon his failure to follow up his victory at Dresden. Caulain-

THE WILL AS MIND 145

court explains that "The Emperor was ill." (III, III, i, 378) Napoleon is so weary at Leipzig that he falls asleep while dictating an order for retreat. As he seeks to escape the city, he is "haggard and in disordered attire." A citizen who sees him mingle with the crowd describes him as "soiled," "inert," and in a "lax mood." (III, III, v, 390-391)

When Napoleon is defeated, deserted, and forced to abdicate, the Spirit of the Years says, "How heavily grinds the Will upon his brain,/His halting hand, and his unlighted eye." This image of reluctant gears directly connects Napoleon's physical condition with the difficulty of the Will in manipulating him. Napoleon speaks of his own mind at this time as a "flaccid brain." (III, IV, iv, 414) When Napoleon is ill, despondent, or weary, he cannot do what the Will urges.

Perhaps his rest on Elba enables the Will to reassert Its sway. Genius guides his magnificent swoop through France. But Napoleon overestimates what he can do. His body is less fit than it was; a stage direction says that Napoleon, as he leaves Elba, "is much fatter than when he left France." (III, V, i, 430)

At Waterloo, Hardy's emphasis upon the impediment of Napoleon's body to the operation of the Will cannot be misunderstood. The swoop through France was too much for him. He falls asleep at Charleroi, and his Secretary says, "These eighteen hours/He's been astride; and is not what he was." He wakes to hear depressing news, that Marie Louise had no retort when Archduke John expressed the hope that Napoleon might be "run through,/Or shot, or break his neck, for your own good." He says "Bah!" to a letter signed "The Duke of Enghien!"—long dead—but when he falls asleep, he dreams of "hundreds of thousands of skeletons and corpses in various stages of decay. They rise from his various battlefields, the flesh dropping from them, and gaze reproachfully at him. . . . In front is the DUKE OF ENGHIEN as showman." He cries out in his sleep and "jumps up in a sweat." (III, VI, iii, 466-468)

Naturally, he is in a bad mood as the battle of Waterloo opens. He looks through a glass, his face a "gloomy resentful countenance, blue-black where shaven, and stained with snuff, with powderings of the same on the breast of his uniform. His stumpy figure . . . accentuates his stoutness." (III, VII, ii, 487) At a crisis in the battle, Napoleon "nods in momentary sleep," during which he dreams of Lannes, "just as he looked/That day at Aspern: mutilated, bleeding!" Ney, whose magnificent assaults have come "Within an ace/Of breaking

THE WILL AS MIND

down the English," sends for help. Napoleon would like to help: " 'Twould write upon the sunset 'Victory!'/But whom may spare we from the right here now?/No single man!" The single man who had saved the day in earlier battles was Napoleon. At Wagram, the Emperor Francis says, "Bonaparte,/By reckless riskings of his life and limb,/Has turned the steelyard of our strength to-day." (II, IV, iii, 242) But the thought does not occur to Napoleon now. He only says, "Life's curse begins, I see,/With helplessness!" Making some minor redispositions to support Ney, Napoleon says, "Further than this/None but the Gods can scheme!" (III, VII, vi, 501-504)

The implications of this scene are that Napoleon's ability to scheme as "Gods can scheme" forsook him. Hardy clearly intended to suggest that the Will could not guide Napoleon because he was weary and depressed. The point is underscored, as it were, by Wellington's comment in the following scene:

> Manoeuvring does not seem to animate
> Napoleon's methods now. Forward he comes,
> And pounds away on us in the ancient style,
> Till he is beaten back in the ancient style.
> (III, VII, vii, 505)

The failure occurs at the crisis of the battle. In Hardy's interpretation, Napoleon's weariness and depression so impede the clairvoyant Mind in him that he loses the battle of Waterloo.

(4) Conscious resistance to the Will to defeat Its purposes or alter Its effects requires that one have Schopenhauer's and Von Hartmann's concept of the Will. The characters in *The Dynasts* who have this concept are the Spirits: they see the Will made visible. The Spirit of the Pities resists the Will vigorously. The Shade of the Earth protests the way of the Will when Maria Louisa agrees to wed Napoleon. Earth protests the acts of the Will against nature, so to speak, in the carnage at Borodino: "The fumes of nitre and the reek of gore/Make my airs foul and fulsome unto me!" (III, I, v, 344)

People in the Napoleonic period did not see the Will as Hardy saw It. Hardy could not have his human characters echo Von Hartmann in resisting the Will. But there is some conscious resistance to Its impulses among the human characters.

Certainly the contemplation of suicide is resistance to the Will. In the struggle of the Spirit of the Pities and the Spirit of the Years to influence Villeneuve, the Spirit of the Years as spokesman for the Will voiced "stern Nays," Villeneuve says, "At each unhappy time I

THE WILL AS MIND 149

strove to pass." Villeneuve meditates the Spirit of the Pities' suggestion that "no percipience here" is "far better." Then the Spirit of the Years tells him that the nays "Have been annulled." (I, V, vi, 105) The scene suggests that Villeneuve's pain and the Spirit of the Pities' suggestion enable Villeneuve to overcome impulses from the Will.

Napoleon seems to resist impulses from the Will at the birth of his son. The physician DuBois tells Napoleon that he cannot save both the Empress and the unborn child. He asks, "Which life is to be saved?" Clearly the Will that made Napoleon marry to plant an heir upon his throne would save the child. But Napoleon has loved the Empress, and from that feeling comes his reply: "Then save the mother, pray! Think but of her;/It is her privilege and my command." When the physician tells Napoleon that "The child is dead," Napoleon's feeling does not waver. He replies: "Praise Heaven for that!/I'll not grieve overmuch about the child."

The comment of the Ironic Chorus upon this scene indicates Hardy's point to be that Napoleon's resistance swayed the Will:

> The Will Itself is slave to him,
> And holds it blissful to obey!—
> . . . .

> The Will grew conscious at command,
> And ordered issue as he planned.
> (II, VI, iii, 293-298)

Beyond these examples, it may be considered that every generous, selfless action in the drama expresses resistance to the selfish, egocentric impulses of the Immanent Will. For example, Nelson is a compassionate man, with no ambitions for himself. He is not rash like those made mad by the Will, but he places other values above his life. He insists on wearing his decorations during the battle of Trafalgar: "They were awarded to me as an honour,/And shall I do despite to those who prize me,/And slight their gifts?" Told that wearing his honors may cost his life, he says, "I would not hide a button/To save ten lives like mine." When he has been fatally wounded, he tries to send the doctor away to others: "Doctor, I'm gone. I am waste o' time to you." (I, V, ii, 85-88) Told that the man who shot him has been killed, he says:

> He was, no doubt, a man
> Who in simplicity and sheer good faith
> Strove but to serve his country. Rest be to him!
> And may his wife, his friends, his little ones,
> If such he had, be tided through their loss,
> And soothed amid the sorrow brought by me.
> (I, V, iv, 95)

THE WILL AS MIND

Though the Will is not named, Nelson's behavior is conscious and even stubborn resistance to the impulses for self that flow from It.

Resistance has not visibly changed the Will at the end of the drama. But the clash of opinion among the Spirits reaches the conclusion that in the future of "far-ranged aions" it may do so.

CHAPTER FOUR

Hardy's Evolutionary Meliorism

"CONSCIOUSNESS THE WILL INFORMING"
> Part is mine of the general Will,
> Cannot my share in the sum of sources
> Bend a digit the poise of forces,
> And a fair desire fulfil?[1]

THESE CONCLUDING lines of Hardy's poem "He Wonders About Himself" suggest one of the propositions underlying Hardy's evolutionary meliorism in *The Dynasts*. The poem is dated November, 1893. This fact may help solve the puzzle of the extent to which Hardy's meliorism is original. As pointed out in Chapter One, Hardy stated in a letter to Edward Wright: "That the Unconscious Will of the Universe is growing aware of Itself I believe I may claim as my own idea solely—at which I arrived by reflecting that what has already taken place in a fraction of the whole . . . is likely to take place in the mass." On the other hand, Hardy

1. *Collected Poems*, p. 480.

told William Archer that Von Hartmann's *Philosophy of the Unconscious* "suggested to me . . . that there may be a consciousness, infinitely far off, at the other end of the chain of phenomena, always striving to express itself." The fusion of the idea in "He Wonders About Himself" and the idea of a consciousness striving to express itself forms the basis for Hardy's evolutionary meliorism.

I do not suppose it possible to discover when Hardy read Von Hartmann. His copy of the *Philosophy of the Unconscious* was the 1893 edition, but he may not have read it before he wrote the poem. I suppose he did not. On the other hand, his statement to Archer and the evident similarity of his ideas to Von Hartmann's indicate Hardy's reliance upon the philosopher for development of his meliorism. Now, Hardy said that Von Hartmann "suggested" the theory of a consciousness striving to express itself. This statement, acceptable in a conversation, cannot be literally true. Brought up in the Church, Hardy knew the Christian concept that God seeks to express His will in the world. What Hardy, who rejected the authority of Divine revelation, must have meant is that Von Hartmann provided him with bases in scientific and philosophic thought for believing probable the development of a universal consciousness—a Cosmic Mind. If he wrote "He Wonders About Himself" before he read Von Hartmann, Hardy had already surmised that an individual desire is part of a "general Will" and might influence Its volitions. Then Von Hartmann provided him a structure of systematic thought to support this surmise. If this explanation is close to the truth, then there is basis for Hardy's claim to originality, even if his statements blur just what was original. As the following discussion shows, Hardy's "own idea solely" is that when the Mind becomes conscious, It may fulfil a fair desire. This idea, which differs from Von Hartmann's conclusion and which forms the climax of *The Dynasts,* is stated as a question in the poem of 1893.

No doubt the idea of the "general Will' reflects Hardy's reading of Schopenhauer. Perhaps Hardy's idea that human desire might alter the dispensations of this Will reflects his residue of Christian feeling. The difference between Hardy's idea and ordinary faith in prayer seems to be that Hardy could not believe God to be a personality. Hardy found his intellectual denial that God is a Person supported by Von Hartmann's reasoning. Von Hartmann observes that to believe in the concept of the Mind as a personality may be a dangerous distortion, employed with the intention of "smuggling in unsuitable ideas" because they are "perhaps consoling to the heart."[2] The Spirit of the Pities exhibits just this tendency when the Spirit of the Years asks what he would hope the Will to be. A Semichorus of the Pities paeans It as a personality: "Great and Good, Thee, Thee we hail." (After Scene, p. 522) But the Pities abandon this hope when the Spirit of the Years says that it cannot be a fact. In the later song expressing Hardy's meliorism, Choruses of the Pities call the Will "It." At any rate, the idea that human desire may influence even a non-personal Will appears in the poem of 1893.

Von Hartmann's contribution to Hardy's meliorism is the support of scientific and philosophic reasoning for the idea that consciousness, developing in living beings, may gradually so prevail through the universe that the Mind may become conscious.

Von Hartmann says that in primitive life-forms the neural organization (or brain) is unconscious. The developing brain responds to stimuli long before it becomes reflectively conscious. Consciousness arises when the brain perceives external stimuli as sensations, and consciousness develops as the brain reflects upon

2. Von Hartmann, II, 261.

them. Von Hartmann considers whether consciousness may have some other origin. We may suppose "consciousness as a product of the unconscious mind and the material action on the same; *or* we divide the whole system of mental activity between Materialism and Spiritualism in such a way that the conscious spirit belongs to the former, the unconscious to the latter, *i. e.,* we assume that the unconscious mind indeed has a self-dependent existence independent of matter, but that the conscious mind is an exclusive product of material processes without any co-operation of unconscious mind." The alternative "is not difficult to decide," for "The essential similarity of conscious and unconscious mental action alone causes a fundamentally different origin for both to appear unthinkable."[3] The point is that consciousness arises from processes that are unconscious.

Von Hartmann discusses at length the idea that the development of consciousness is the "goal of evolution." *"By the way of the unfolding of consciousness* must then the goal of evolution be sought, and consciousness is beyond a doubt the *proximate* end of Nature—of the world. The question still remains open whether consciousness is really *ultimate end,*

3. *Ibid.*, II, 81.

EVOLUTIONARY MELIORISM 157

therefore also self-end, or whether it again serves only *another* end?"⁴

The idea that the Unconscious may develop consciousness in itself as a whole is suggested all through the *Philosophy of the Unconscious*. Beginning with the premise that in the Unconscious "Will and idea are united . . . in an inseparable unity," Von Hartmann describes what happens when the world-process develops consciousness in the individual:

> Then organised matter suddenly breaks in upon this self-contained peace of the Unconscious, and in the reaction of sensation occurring according to necessary laws thrusts upon the astonished individual spirit an idea which falls upon it as from the skies, for it finds in itself no will to this idea. For the first time "the matter of intuition is given to it from without." The great revolution has come to pass, the first step to the world's redemption taken; the idea has been rent from the will, to confront it in future as an independent power, in order to bring under subjection to itself its former lord. This amazement of the will at the rebellion against its previously acknowledged sway, this sensation which the interloping idea produces in the Unconscious, this is *Consciousness*.⁵

In developing consciousness in its creatures, the Unconscious creates pain. Hardy sees this fact as a flaw in the process. As the Shade of the Earth says, that men "feel, and puppetry

4. *Ibid.*, III, 122.
5. *Ibid.*, II, 82-84.

remain,/Is an owned flaw in her consistency/ Men love to dub Dame Nature." (I, I, vi, 34) The Spirit of the Pities cries out at "the intolerable antilogy/Of making figments feel!" and the Ironic Spirit agrees that "Logic's in that." (I, IV, v, 77)

Since the creatures of the Unconscious that become conscious of pain are its phenomena and parts of it, the Unconscious experiences pain. Von Hartmann says that the pain it feels does not swerve it, if the pain is necessary in the process of development: "the Unconscious can be led astray neither more nor less by the lamentation of milliards of human individuals than by that of as many animal individuals, if only these torments further *development,* and thereby its own main design."[6]

Von Hartmann asks whether the Unconscious, having created consciousness and pain, drives on toward further consciousness as a means of relieving this pain, whether "the all-knowing Unconscious thinking end and means at once has created consciousness *for that very reason, to redeem the will from the unblessedness of its willing,* from which it cannot redeem itself," and whether "the real end of the world-process, to which consciousness serves as final means, *is this, to realise the greatest possible*

6. *Ibid.,* II, 13.

attainable state of happiness, namely, that of painlessness?"[7] Von Hartmann surmises that the Will made conscious would relieve pain by ceasing to will and hence to exist—that is, by annihilation of the world. He suggests that this is the only way the Unconscious may achieve this end: "Were now this end *attainable without consciousness,* or did such a consciousness in the sense of an emancipation of the Idea from the will exist at the beginning of the world-process in God, the whole cosmic process would be *foolish* and *aimless,* in that it would be struggling to attain somewhat that either is *not at all requisite* for the object, or that *existed long ago.*"[8]

Von Hartmann thought that man's reason might aid the Unconscious in its effort to find redemption in annihilation. Many passages express this idea: "Unquestionably, besides its value for the individual as such, consciousness has also in addition a universal significance for the redemption of the world, *i. e.,* for the conversion of the World Will and its return to the original condition before the commencement of the world-process . . . ; for this final purpose the All-One does in fact need consciousness, and accordingly it possesses the same,—namely,

7. *Ibid.,* III, 125.
8. *Ibid.,* II, 274-275.

in the sum of individual consciousnesses, whose common subject it is."[9] Man, in helping to make the Unconscious aware, contributes to this redemption. This, in Von Hartmann's thought, is the way the world ends: "The logical principle guides the world-process most wisely to the goal of the greatest possible evolution of consciousness, which being attained, consciousness suffices to hurl back the total actual volition into nothingness, by which the *process* and the *world ceases,* and ceases indeed without any residuum whatever whereby the process might be continued."[10] Hardy reflects Von Hartmann's thought in the fear of the Spirit Sinister that the Spirit Ironic may "wake up the Unconscious Itself, and tempt It to let all the gory clock-work of the show run down." (II, IV, v, 245)

This reasoning suggests that for the individual suicide may be desirable. Schopenhauer thought the nature of the Will unchangeable, and man's only hope for escaping the pain of life a saintly renunciation of the Will—a suicide of the senses, at least. Hardy was probably serious in considering renunciation and even suicide as at least philosophically superior to the endurance of the world as it is, if there be no hope for its amelioration. The Spirit of the

9. *Ibid.,* II, 250. 10. *Ibid.,* III, 142.

EVOLUTIONARY MELIORISM 161

Pities, evidently speaking for Hardy, suggests suicide to Villeneuve. Observing the suffering of the soldiers dying at Albuera, a Chorus of the Pities prays to Earth to "Hide their hacked bones, Earth!" for "Better than waking is to sleep!" (II, VI, iv, 302) In the conclusion of *The Dynasts*, following the question whether Its blindness shall break and Its heart awake, a Chorus of the Pities sings:

> Should It never
> Curb or cure
> Aught whatever
> Those endure
> Whom It quickens, let them darkle to extinction swift and sure. (After Scene, p. 525)

But that It would never curb or cure was not Hardy's conclusion!

In order for consciousness to modify the world-process, the will must be free. Human beings must have freedom of the will to act as taught by reason, and the Will must have freedom to alter Its courses. Freedom of the will means freedom to choose between one or the other of two bases for action.

One basis for human action is the volitions of the Will, which flow into the individual mind as instinct, desire, and impulse. But consciousness provides a second basis. From the external world sensations flow into the individual's brain and there produce awareness, feeling, and reflection. Conscious reflection allows man to choose on the basis of reason instead of impulse. Since there are two bases for action, then, (1) impulses of the Immanent Will and (2) reflection of the mind upon sensations from the external world, some freedom of the will is possible.

If this is a fair statement of Hardy's reasoning, he found support for it in the *Philosophy of the Unconscious*. Von Hartmann said that the impulses of the Unconscious which activate the will need not pass through the conscious mind: "it is somewhat *accidental to the will,* whether it passes through the *cerebral* consciousness or not."[11] The Will thus brings about actions that are not produced by reflection, or as Hardy said in his final display of the Will, men act while discovering their intention to act. (III, VII, vii, 505) But men may act on the basis of "the conscious idea," which, Von Hartmann said, "is a product of . . . the cerebral vibrations" produced by perception.[12] For actions that result from perception and reflection, Von Hartmann used the specific term *freewill,* saying: "to distinguish the two kinds of will, for conscious will language already offers a term exactly covering this conception—

11. *Ibid.*, I, 69.   12. *Ibid.*, II, 61.

EVOLUTIONARY MELIORISM 163

Freewill—. . . Will, we know, is the resultant of all contemporaneous desires; if this struggle of desire is consciously waged, it appears as a choice of the result, or freewill."[13] In this way, as Swann pointed out in discussing Von Hartmann, man "under the joint control of will and reason" has some freedom, and "this is substantially Hardy's position."[14]

To Hardy, freedom of the will is therefore freedom *from* the Will—from instincts and selfish desires. It is freedom to choose the objects suggested by the rational mind and compassion. But this freedom is limited: the impulses of the Will are strongly compulsive. The limits are suggested in the struggle between the Spirit of the Pities and the Spirit of the Years to influence Villeneuve. Villeneuve is moved by facts like his "rotten . . . marine." As he debates whether to follow Napoleon's command or face his rage, Villeneuve writes "ambiguous lines/That facts have forced from me." His compassion is stirred by psychic messages from the Spirit of the Pities—"apprehensions" from "some influence." The Spirit of the Years, as channel of the Will, tugs him in the opposite direction, till the Spirit of the Pities chides the

13. *Ibid.*, I, 69.
14. George Rogers Swann, *Philosophical Parallelisms in Six English Novelists,* Philadelphia: University of Pennsylvania, 1929, p. 28.

Spirit of the Years. This Spirit replies that he must torment Villeneuve, for, he says, "I know but narrow freedom./. . . as he." (I, II, ii, 42-43) Though strongly moved to defy Napoleon, Villeneuve is able only to hesitate and swerve—enough indeed to check Napoleon's invasion of England—before his desperate gamble at Trafalgar. The struggle goes on within him, after Trafalgar, between suicide and the will to survive. He wants to kill himself; the Spirit of the Pities urges him to do so. But he cannot until the Will gives permission. This is indeed "narrow freedom."

That Hardy held this theory of a limited freedom of the will and believed that *The Dynasts* made his position clear is evident from his letters. Writing to Edward Wright, in 1907, Hardy said that his theory set forth in *The Dynasts* "seems to me to settle the question of Free-Will v. Necessity. The will of a man is, according to it, neither wholly free nor wholly unfree. When swayed by the Universal Will . . . he is not individually free; but whenever it happens that all the rest of the Great Will is in equilibrium the minute portion called one person's will is free, just as a performer's fingers are free to go on playing the pianoforte of themselves when . . . the head does not rule

EVOLUTIONARY MELIORISM 165

them."[15] Hardy wrote similarly to Dr. Caleb Saleeby in 1914: "The nature of the determination embraced in the theory is that of a collective will; so that there is a proportion of the total will in each part of the whole, and each part has therefore, in strictness, *some* freedom, which would, in fact, be operative as such whenever the remaining great mass of will in the universe should happen to be in equilibrium."[16] The repeated phrase "in equilibrium" seems to indicate a "poise of forces" possible when the impulses of the Will are felt weakly. They are strong in passion or frenzy. They are weakened when they are impeded by weariness or other listlessness of the human brain; and they are resisted by impulses that arise from full consciousness (reflective reason) or compassion strong enough to establish a poise of forces.

Freedom within narrow limits seems to be suggested by speculations in parapsychology, where it is reported that one warned by a dream or a feeling of coming disaster may avert the disaster—in this way altering a seemingly predestined future.[17] Possibly Hardy had something of this kind in mind when he portrayed the death of Sir Thomas Picton. Picton saw his death-phantom as he left the Duchess of

15. *The Later Years*, p. 125.   16. *Ibid.*, pp. 269-270.
17. See footnote 36 of Chapter Three.

Richmond's ball. Frenzied on the field of Waterloo, he is warned by a voice against his rashness. He does *not* heed the warning, cries "What the hell care I?" rides conspicuously onward, and falls dead with a bullet in his forehead. (III, VII, ii, 490) Presumably Picton had the freedom to ride less conspicuously and avoid at least the particular bullet that hit him. But, made frantic by the Will, this man who "coolly conned and drily spoke" to his death-phantom could not coolly choose.

That the human will is sufficiently free to allow man to act on the basis of reason and compassion does not necessarily mean that the Immanent Will is similarly free. Schopenhauer's Will is free, for it creates its own laws. But Hardy's Will is more like Von Hartmann's Unconscious, which is a Mind dreaming a dream. In *The Dynasts,* the Spirit of the Years insists that the Will is restricted by "rapt aesthetic rote" in the operation of Its "clock-like laws." (Fore Scene, p. 1) But this is the Spirit of the Years speaking for scientific determinism—not Hardy. Hardy speculated that some freedom in the individual implies some freedom in the total Will. If It is outside space and time, and Its dream is contained within It like pictures on a motion-picture film, can It change the future in any detail? Perhaps the

EVOLUTIONARY MELIORISM 167

general shape of the immediate, "foreseeable" future is fixed by causes already operative, but perhaps the far-distant future may be subject to rearrangements by causes not yet operative. If the Will as Mind has unconscious precognition (contains the knowledge, without awareness of it) that consciousness may develop, perhaps It has (as Von Hartmann suggested) chosen this process for Its redemption. Perhaps this knowledge is a variable in Its equations. Hardy supposed the Will has purpose in the sense of general direction. But the Will may swerve from Its predestined course under the pressure of an "outside" force like consciousness, as an automobile plunging down a straight highway may be slightly swerved by the wind. Its general purpose, say, evolutionary development, continues, but man through compassion may treasure and save what the Will alone might destroy as unfit to survive.

The outside force that may swerve the Will is man's consciousness, man's exercise of his limited freedom, and hence man's pressure upon the Will. The individual man is an almost infinitesimal "digit" in the "poise of forces," but each has "parcel" in the whole. As the Will is immanent in man, so is man within It, and man's consciousness informs the Mind of what It did not know—wakens in It a tiny area of awareness. To this minute extent, man is a variable in the equations of the Will's determinism. The generations come and pass like drops of rain, but they continue on and on. The Spirit of the Pities as representative of man's compassion that may grow through all time would seem to be a channel for man's influence upon the Will. The Spirit of the Years and the Spirit Ironic jeer the Spirit of the Pities' attempts to pray, but seem to join him in a song of hope at the end of the drama.

To the extent that the Mind may be free to wake gradually to consciousness through the aid of the human mind, It needs that aid. Its processes are mechanical, even though It is alive and has the potential for developing consciousness and moral values. It needs man's help to redeem Itself from mechanism.

Hardy was certainly familiar with J. S. Mill's idea that, even if God is a "Principle of Good," He "*cannot* at once and altogether subdue the powers of evil," and "man's duty would consist . . . in standing forth a not ineffectual auxiliary to a Being of perfect beneficence."[18] Von Hartmann did not think of the Unconscious as good. The impulses of consciousness are

---

18. John Stuart Mill, *Three Essays on Religion: Nature, The Utility of Religion, and Theism*, London: Longmans, Green, etc., 1874, p. 39.

morally higher than those from the Unconscious: "action from consciousness may be regulated according to principles which reason dictates. . . . Wherever consciousness is able to replace the Unconscious, it *ought* to replace it, just because it is to the individual the higher."[19] Man's pressure upon the Mind, then, would help It to consciousness and morality. Weber suggests that this idea of man's duty to inform and aid the cosmic process toward realization of moral values runs throughout the Wessex novels. "Man can and must accept responsibility for maintaining values, humane values, and must exert himself in carrying out this responsibility with the greate. determination and energy, *just because* he finds moral values missing in the cosmos."[20] Hardy's more specific concept in *The Dynasts* resembles that recently phrased by Montague. Montague says that it is man's duty to regard the Cosmic Mind "not as a King of kings but as a Comrade of comrades, needing our aid as we need his in that unending pursuit of the ideal which for God no less than for Man makes up the meaning of existence."[21] Certainly the

19. Von Hartmann, II, 41.
20. Carl J. Weber, *Hardy in America: A Study of Thomas Hardy and His American Readers*, Waterville, Maine: Colby College Press, 1946, p. 180.
21. William Pepperell Montague, "Does the Universe Have a Mind?" *The Saturday Review of Literature*, XXX (September 6, 1947), 32.

idea that man's consciousness ought to inform the Mind of moral, humane values runs through *The Dynasts* to the climactic last line of the play.

In many of his poems also, Hardy expressed this idea that man ought to inform the Mind of humane values. In "The Lacking Sense" of 1901, he urges Man to help the groping Mother (Nature): "while she plods dead-reckoning on, in darkness of affliction,/Assist her where thy creaturely dependence can or may,/ For thou art of her clay."[22] In "God's Education," God muses that men teach God the meaning of mercy: "The thought is new to me./ Forsooth, though I men's master be,/Theirs is the teaching mind."[23]

These ideas are no mere fantasies. Brennecke, though justly tracing a good deal of Hardy's thought to Schopenhauer, is mistaken in calling Hardy's evolutionary meliorism a "rather vaguely defined hope or faith" that takes three general forms: "the Nirwana of non-existence, the growth of consciousness in the Will, and a melioristic belief in a gradual improvement in life through the idealistic efforts of enlightened men."[24] There is nothing

22. *Collected Poems*, p. 107.
23. *Ibid.*, p. 262.
24. Ernest Brennecke, Jr., *Thomas Hardy's Universe: A Study of a Poet's Mind*, London: T. Fisher Unwin, 1924, p. 141.

"vaguely defined" in Hardy's meliorism. Point by point: (1) Here and there the poetry and *The Dynasts* do meditate "the Nirwana of non-existence," but it is not a part of Hardy's meliorism. It is an alternative to amelioration; it is desirable only if the Mind may "never/Curb or cure" the needless pain It inflicts. (2) The "growth of consciousness in the Will" is expressed in lyric imagery, but it is not vague. It is especially clear when we lay aside Schopenhauer's concept of Reality as Will and observe Von Hartmann's concept of Reality as Mind.[25] (3) The "gradual improvement in life through the idealistic efforts of enlightened men" is linked with Hardy's evolutionary meliorism as a means in the process, for enlightened men inform the Mind. Hardy defines their role in his "Apology" in *Late Lyrics and Earlier*: "whether the human and kindred animal races survive till the exhaustion or destruction of

25. This concept would not seem vague to a twentieth-century scientist. Sir James Jeans says, for example: "To-day there is a wide measure of agreement, which on the physical side of science approaches almost to unanimity, that the stream of knowledge is heading towards a non-mechanical reality; the universe begins to look more like a great thought than like a great machine. Mind no longer appears as an accidental intruder into the realm of matter; we are beginning to suspect that we ought rather to hail it as the creator and governor of the realm of matter—not of course our individual minds, but the mind in which the atoms out of which our individual minds have grown exist as thoughts." Sir James Jeans, *The Mysterious Universe*, New York: The Macmillan Company, 1931, p. 158.

the globe . . . pain to all upon it, tongued or dumb, shall be kept down to a minimum by loving-kindness, operating through scientific knowledge, and actuated by the modicum of free will conjecturally possessed by organic life when the mighty necessitating forces . . . happen to be in equilibrium, which may or may not be often."[26]

Hardy's reasoning to support the idea that the Mind may grow conscious is expressed in an analogy spoken by the Spirit of the Pities: "Men gained cognition with the flux of time,/ And wherefore not the Force informing them . . . ?" (After Scene, p. 522) Its cognition is through the individual's "share in the sum of sources" that cumulatively and at last is sufficient to "Bend a digit the poise of forces." Human pain and even prayer may affect It. When the Spirit of the Pities seeks to pray "To some Great Heart" and the Ironic Chorus asks where "Its compassions sit?" the play as a whole suggests an answer. Its compassions abide in men's feelings, and to pray is to shape a minute portion of It, so that—to the extent of that portion—It "haply may/Charm mortal miseries away!" (II, VI, v, 306)

This process of evolutionary meliorism may take place in two stages, as a Chorus of the

26. *Collected Poems*, p. 527.

Pities says: "Nay;—shall not Its blindness break?/Yea, must not Its heart awake . . . ?" (After Scene, p. 525)

The first of the stages is awareness, the breaking of blindness. Hardy saw the emergence of consciousness as an accident of evolution; as the Spirit of the Years says, no "cognizance has marshalled things terrene." (Fore Scene, p. 2) Yet It may learn from Its own experience in Its parts that suffer experience. The Spirits discuss this point throughout the play. In the Fore Scene, the Spirit of the Pities asks whether the impact of experience upon men's minds—"Sublunar shocks"—may wake the Mind. If It were wakened, the Mind would see Its creation as "ill-contrived," for it is the breaking of "nescience" that enables the Spirit to see this fact. (II, IV, vii, 250) He believes that the "unscanted scope" of the Mind "Affords a food for final Hope,/That mild-eyed Prescience ponders nigh/Life's loom." (After Scene, p. 523)[27]

The role of man's intelligence in waking the Mind to perception of absurdity is symbolized by the Spirit Ironic. When the weary soldiers on both sides at Talavera drink together as alike "earth's sojourners" and then retire to

27. In the first version *Prescience ponders nigh* is given as *Consciousness stands nigh*. (American edition, p. 351.) Both *Consciousness* and the *ponders* that goes with *Prescience* express the idea that awareness is the first step toward amelioration.

shoot at one another, the Spirit Ironic comments upon the absurdity of "Life's queer mechanics." The absurdity is so evident that the Spirit Sinister expresses fear that the Spirit Ironic may wake up "the Unconscious Itself." Von Hartmann had suggested that if the Unconscious should come to see such absurdities "with open eyes" It would not allow them to continue. He said, "Incomprehensible and unpardonable as the first commencement would be without the hypothesis of a blind action, no less incomprehensible and unpardonable would be the *laisser-aller* of this misery with open eyes."[28] In Von Hartmann's thought, awareness would lead It to annihilate the world, or, as the Spirit Sinister puts it, to let the "gory clock-work . . . run down." (II, IV, v, 245) But Hardy supposed that awareness might lead the Mind to reform Its ill-contrived creation. For example, as he stated in his conversation with Archer, war is doomed to come to an end "because of its absurdity."

The second stage is the waking of the heart—the development of compassion as a consequence of awareness. Hardy meditated this point in his notebook for March-April, 1890: "Altruism, or The Golden Rule, or whatever 'Love your Neighbor as Yourself' may be called,

---

28. Von Hartmann, II, 274.

will ultimately be brought about I think by the pain we see in others reacting on ourselves, as if we and they were a part of one body."[29] Von Hartmann made the same observation in just the form in which it is developed in *The Dynasts:* "Now compassion arises by way of reflection through the sensuous perception of another's suffering. . . . For example, when we read of a battle where ten thousand dead and wounded are counted on either side, we are scarcely at all affected, only when the dead and wounded are summoned before our imagination does our compassion stir; but when we ourselves go about among the pools of blood, the corpses and the limbs, and the groaning and dying men, then indeed a deep horror overcomes us." Furthermore, Von Hartmann continued, compassion leads to what Hardy calls loving-kindness: "What value the instinct of compassion has for man, who only through mutual help truly becomes man, is tolerably plain. . . . it is the most significant impulse for the begetting of such actions as consciousness declares to be morally good or beautiful."[30] In *The Dynasts,* the stoic Spirit of the Years is inclined to view human affairs aloofly, in terms of the facts about the "ten thousand dead and wounded."

29. *The Early Life,* p. 294.
30. Von Hartmann, I, 210-211.

The Spirit of the Pities wishes to move the Spirit of the Years to compassion and so invites him to suffer with men by becoming a man for a while, "donning their poor mould." As compassion is a human trait, an evolution subsequent to awareness, the juvenile Spirit of the Pities has yet made no perceptible impression on the Mind. But he may do so, for in incarnating Itself, the Immanent Mind may become conscious of pain within Itself.

Then through man's help, informed by man's awareness and compassion, the Mind may bring about "The Great Adjustment."[31] It may not be a miraculous awakening of the Mind, with abrupt alteration of natural law—if indeed alteration of natural law at all—as to establish perpetual springtime. Hardy has been misunderstood on this point. Miss Garwood, comparing Von Hartmann's concept with Hardy's, says of this adjustment that "in the philosopher this consciousness is to be consummated in the race, in the author we get the impression that it is to occur outside the race and come to men as an effect of change, rather than as a process of change."[32] Chakravarty's statement

[31] See "There Seemed a Strangeness," *Collected Poems*, p. 689.

[32] Helen Garwood, *Thomas Hardy: An Illustration of the Philosophy of Schopenhauer*, Philadelphia: Winston, 1911 (University of Pennsylvania doctoral dissertation), p. 79.

EVOLUTIONARY MELIORISM 177

is closer to the truth. He says, "Nature will go on 'pressing change on change' . . . Nature itself will not necessarily improve, but . . . human consciousness may well take up the implied challenge of Nature. . . . the conditions of humanity will not advance till our emotions, not content merely with appeals of prayer or suffering, begin also to try to put prayers into concrete form, into preventive, remedial, and creative actions."[33] Men "in fair compassions skilled,/. . . . who love the true, the excellent" may bring about the change without apparent help from the laws of nature, for, as the Shade of the Earth says, "I am not averse." (Fore Scene, p. 3) In short, it is not outside nature's laws as they stand or the possibilities of earth for the Mind operating in men to "fashion all things fair."

The Mind made conscious would not be passive. Its measure of consciousness would lie within Its conscious parts, grown more and more numerous and prevalent with the passage of the ages. Informed by the human mind, It would operate, as It now operates, within the human mind. Its "Lisbon earthquakes," as irremediable ills, might still continue, but within Its conscious parts, men's minds, It

[33]. Amiya Chakravarty, *THE DYNASTS and the Post-War Age in Poetry*, London, New York, Toronto: Oxford University Press, 1938, p. 40.

would gradually weaken the impulses underlying selfishness and cruelty. Whether or not Hardy had in mind the song of a Chorus in *The Drama of Kings,* the process he described resembles it: "God works within all wrongs, and wastes indeed/The secret force on which they live and feed;/This being withdrawn, they die and disappear."[34]

When I consider Hardy's meaning, I do not see the difference that Miss Garwood sees between Von Hartmann's concept—"consciousness . . . consummated in the race"— and Hardy's, except that Hardy, to dramatize the change, had the Spirit of the Pities sum up in a poetic image an evolution stated to extend through vast ages. Von Hartmann describes how the Mind operates within human life to bring about change suitable to it in these words: "The Unconscious must (apart from its continuous interposition in every organic formation, thus also in all generation) display a direct activity in the progressive development of the organisation: on the one hand, in order with new germs *to call forth* the variations that do *not accidentally* arise, and, on the other hand, to *preserve* from being *again obliterated* by crossing the variations that have arisen, which

---

34. Robert Buchanan, *The Drama of Kings,* London: Strahan & Co., 1871, p. 104.

belong to its plan."[35] Von Hartmann stresses this point that the activity of the Unconscious is most evident in the pivots of evolution, that is, in the areas of generation. Hardy reflects this very idea. The Spirit Sinister notes that the Will designed the "rare dramas" of the Napoleonic wars when "It wove Its web in that Ajaccian womb!" of Napoleon's mother. (Fore Scene, p. 2) Hardy again suggests the interposition of the Will in the processes of generation when he has Ironic Spirits explain that the Will grew conscious and brought Napoleon's dead son to life at Napoleon's command. At least, within the concept that Hardy dramatizes, the Mind may operate through impulses that are non-material and non-sensuous—so far imperceptible to instruments of the laboratory —but are not nonsense. In these operations, as even the instance of Napoleon's son shows, man's is the teaching mind. In Hardy's concept, the Mind grows conscious indeed, but only as informed by Its conscious parts—not apart from these parcels of Itself. Hardy's meaning, I think, is that when men develop

35. Von Hartmann, II, 330. To the extent that the Mind operates through the processes being investigated by parapsychologists, It operates in "a world of causality new to science. . . . Its operations, though imperceptible to the senses, are nonetheless energetically real, since results that are discoverable are produced." (J. B. Rhine, *New World of the Mind*, New York: William Sloane, 1953, pp. 119-120.)

compassion and strive to establish a kindlier race in a better world, their desire may influence the Mind as, say, prayer is presumed to influence God, and the Mind, operating through impulses upon life-processes that are slightly variable in the areas of generation—upon mutations—will offer the aid It is free to offer.

There are no walls of Jericho in this concept, tumbling down at the blare of trumpets. Hardy called it *evolutionary* meliorism.[36] The Spirit of the Pities thinks of the process as minutely gradual, to be completed "When far-ranged aions past all fathoming/ Shall have swung by, and stand as backward years." (After Scene, p. 522)

These poetic statements agree with Hardy's opinion stated in his conversation with Archer: "my practical philosophy is distinctly meliorist. . . . Whatever may be the inherent good or evil of life, it is certain that men make it much worse than it need be. When we have got rid of a thousand remediable ills, it will be time enough to determine whether the ill that is irremediable outweighs the good." Archer asked, "And you think that we *are* getting rid of the remediable ills?" Hardy replied, "Slowly

---

[36.] See Hardy's definition in the "Apology" for *Late Lyrics and Earlier, Collected Poems*, pp. 526-527.

but surely—yes."³⁷ In the same year, 1901, Hardy stated this thought in the poem "Agnostoi Theoi." He wonders "How much of consciousness informs" the "Willer masked and dumb." There is no answer: "Nought shows to us ephemeral ones who fill/But moments in Thy mind." But certain elements in human progress suggest that the Will tends "To grow percipient with advance of days,/And with percipience mends." At least, here and there, now and then, "May be discerned a wrong/Dying as of self-slaughter."³⁸

On this basis rests the thrilling final Chorus of *The Dynasts* that assumes the Mind shall³⁹ awake and on awaking mend: man's "Consciousness the Will informing, till It fashion all things fair!"

37. William Archer, "Real Conversations. Conversation 1.— With Mr. Thomas Hardy," *The Critic*, XXXVIII (April, 1901), 316.
38. *Collected Poems*, pp. 171-172.
39. The present tense of "a stirring thrills the air" may be noted. It continues the thought of "Agnostoi Theoi." But of course the final line of *The Dynasts* refers to a gradual process, to be completed in the far-distant future.

CHAPTER FIVE

Napoleon, Servant of the Will

"SUCH A WILL I PASSIVELY OBEYED"

NAPOLEON HAS been called an "example of Hardy's failure with historical character," for Hardy "not only contributes nothing" to the understanding of Napoleon, but "darkens counsel" about him. Hardy "makes us dislike Napoleon, both as an ambitious politician who does not scruple to wade through blood to his own ends, and as an individual who is selfish in his intimate personal relationships, caddish, mean, and even cowardly; while of his greatness we are given no inkling." Rutland, who makes these telling remarks, goes on to consider Hardy's intention: "Either Napoleon was a man, in which case . . . he can be great as well as little . . . or else he was a mere puppet of the Immanent Will. . . . Hardy cannot have it both ways."[1] In my opinion, Hardy did not seek to

1. William R. Rutland, *Thomas Hardy: A Study of His Writings and Their Background*, Oxford: Basil Blackwell, 1938, p. 334.

have it both ways. He does indeed darken counsel about Napoleon as a man, but he does so to illuminate the way of the Will in moulding history. Hardy presents Napoleon as a puppet of the self-centered Will and, in turn, puppet-master of France.

Hardy presents the Napoleonic wars as a violent eruption of the Will operating in history and Napoleon as Its analogue and agent. He sees the man as General Mack of Austria saw him: "not France, but an adventurer/Imposing on that country for his gain." (I, IV, iii, 71) Hardy opens the drama after Napoleon had usurped the French Revolution for his own ends, and he closes it with the Spirit of the Years' evaluation of this adventurer's place in the earthly record. In the scenes between, Hardy selects from the complex exhibitions of Napoleon's character items of behavior that history indeed records, but that blacken Napoleon as a man while illuminating him as a symbol of destructive energy. Besides selection to illustrate the Will, Hardy selects to contrast Napoleon's egoistic genius with Pitt's unselfish service, Fox's exalted sense of honor, and Wellington's cautious certainties.

Rutland presents a number of instances in which Hardy followed first one historian and then another to give historical verisimilitude to his fictional Napoleon. Discussing the divorce scene between Napoleon and Josephine (II, V, ii, 259-267), Rutland points out that Hardy "paraphrased *some* of the recorded words, but discarded other and far more vital ones because they did not fit in with the character which he wished to give to Napoleon." Hardy rejected instances of Napoleon's humane weaknesses: "It would never do for Napoleon to tremble in his whole frame, take his wife's hand, place it on his heart, and say: 'Thou knowest if I have loved thee. To thee, to thee alone do I owe the only moments of happiness which I have enjoyed in this world. . . .' On the other hand, when the history suited the art, Hardy asked nothing better than to be strictly historical."[2] Perhaps a more striking instance of selection to blacken Napoleon is the scene at the battle of Austerlitz when, according to Hardy, Napoleon watches "with a vulpine smile" the Russians fleeing across Satschan lake and "directs a battery near at hand to fire down upon the ice on which the Russians are crossing. . . . Two thousand fugitives are engulfed, and their groans of despair reach the ears of the watchers like ironical huzzas." (I, VI, iv, 121) Some historians suggest this incident; others offer proof that it did not occur,

---

2. *Ibid.*, pp. 293-294.

for when the lake was drained only twenty or so bodies were found in it. Hardy, it seems, chose deliberately, if not to invent, at least to select what suited his intention.

Hardy found the metaphysical basis for his Napoleon in the *Philosophy of the Unconscious*. Von Hartmann's Unconscious moves toward fulfilment of its purpose through natural laws. Evolution, with its principle of survival of the fittest, often the strongest and most ruthless, is one of these laws. It moves toward fulfilment by impelling every individual creature toward the greatest possible self-realization. Each creature in a chain of generations is its temporary mechanism. The larger interest of the will, we may suppose, is human history. Mentioning Napoleon among men whom the Will has used to shape history, Von Hartmann says that "history attains, by the initiative of eminent individuals, results which were quite beside the conscious purposes of such men. (Think in particular of the fertile marriage of different national civilisations . . . even the European revolutions evoked by Napoleon. Only an unhistoric sense can make light of the fields strewed with the corpses of these heroes duped by the Unconscious, whence have sprung harvests so fruitful and rich in blessing.)"[3]

[3.] Von Hartmann, II, 9.

Whatever Hardy thought of the eventual "blessing" of "fields strewed with the corpses," he presents Napoleon as the instrument of the Will. To shape history, It saves Itself expenditure of force by manipulating Napoleon, and he then manipulates history. Von Hartmann states that this is the method of the Will: "As soon as the expenditure of force needed for the setting-up of a machine would become greater than the saving of force attained by the mechanism . . . the direct activity of the Unconscious must display itself without hesitation. Of such a kind are . . . the incursions of the Unconscious in human brains, which . . . guide the course of history . . . in the direction of the goal intended by the Unconscious."[4] Interpretation of Hardy's Napoleon as a mechanism or puppet of the Will and in turn puppet-master of France explains the behavior of Napoleon. Perhaps Hardy was prepared for his concept, seemingly shaped upon Von Hartmann's thought, by his earlier reading of *The Drama of Kings*. In this *Drama* Napoleon speaks of sitting on a throne and seeing "beneath my feet/My puppets sit with strings that reach my hand."[5] In Hardy's concept, the strings reach farther back, to the Will, and only fan out through Napo-

---

4. *Ibid.*, II, 359.

5. Robert Buchanan, *The Drama of Kings*, London: Strahan & Co., 1871, p. 111.

leon. For example, Napoleon's soldiers seem stirred by the Will Itself when he speaks to them. As Napoleon's proclamation is read to the Grand Army departing for Russia, the soldiers "quiver emotionally, like leaves stirred by a wind." (III, I, i, 327) In parallel images that seem intentional, the impulses of the Will are called "winds grown visible" (Fore Scene, p. 7) and "breezes made visible." (III, I, i, 330)

Napoleon as a mechanism of the Will is impelled toward power and command, a goal of the Will, by inner hungers, impulses of the Will. Speaking of genius, Von Hartmann quotes from Schelling that "the man of destiny does not execute what he wills or intends, but what he is obliged to execute through an incomprehensible fate under whose influence he stands."[6] Napoleon's genius, his swift perception of stratagems to outwit his enemies, are direct incursions of the Mind, which always presents the best among the manifold possibilities of a situation. So guided, Napoleon guides "the course of history . . . in the direction of the goal intended by the Unconscious."

To simplify this metaphysical concept, I am calling Napoleon servant of the Will. He is also an analogue of the Will, an illustration of

6. Von Hartmann, I, 280.

Its selfish character. His story parallels even the first stage of Hardy's meliorism in the breaking of awareness into Napoleon's Will-fixed mind, and it prepares for the second stage, the waking of compassion—though Napoleon wards off this development by declaring the Will responsible.

As servant of the Will, Napoleon is subject to Its reasonless and insatiable hungers, chiefly lust for power and command. Whatever dream the historical Napoleon may have had for Europe ultimately unified, ordered for men's good, and at peace, the Napoleon of *The Dynasts* has no such dream except as a means to his own fame. He is possessed by the impulse of the Unconscious that Von Hartmann calls "the lust of power." Of this lust, Von Hartmann says: "There is . . . a passion for commanding and ruling as such. . . . the more one drinks of it, the thirstier one becomes. . . . the love of power is a far more pernicious passion than ambition."[7] Napoleon cares nothing for Villeneuve's sailors, for, as he says, "My brain has only one wish—to succeed!" (I, III, i, 59) To succeed means finally, insatiably, to rule the world. He plots with Russian Alexander to partition the Turkish Empire, so that they "As comrades can conjunctly rule the

---

7. *Ibid.*, III, 56.

world/To its own gain and our eternal fame!" (II, I, viii, 172) but when he receives word that Alexander is about to take the part of Turkey that "I have promised Alexander," Napoleon has another thought: "Ah!.../As for Constantinople being his prize/I'll see him frozen first." (II, III, ii, 213) Thus there are no "comrades . . . conjunctly" in Napoleon's inner scheme, and precious little of the world's "own gain."

In the Fore Scene, the Spirit of the Years defines Napoleon's role as servant of the Will and Napoleon's followers as his puppets. Speaking to the Spirits as "puppet-watchers," the Spirit says:

> You'll mark the twitchings of this Bonaparte
> As he with other figures foots his reel,
> . . . .
> Also regard the frail ones that his flings
> Have made gyrate like animalcula
> In tepid pools. (P. 6)

The figure is a curious one, and it may well, I think, express Hardy's memory of a passage in Von Hartmann describing how the Unconscious, working as instinct, animates a brainless polype in a glass of water. Moved by instinct, the polype "produces a whirlpool with its arms, in order to draw it [an infusorion] within its grasp. . . . The polype then perceives the animalcule to be living . . . and adopts means to bring it within reach of its mouth."[8] Anyway, the figure relates the puppetry to instinct.

Of Napoleon's boasting to General Mack that he can raise vast armies, the Spirit of the Years says in derision, "So let him speak," for the Spirits see that Napoleon is:

> Moved like a figure on a lantern-slide.
> Which . . .
> The all-compelling crystal pane but drags
> Whither the showman wills. (I, IV, v, 76)

Yet, at the end of the drama, the Spirit of the Years bitterly condemns Napoleon, saying that, with all dictators, his place in "Earth's unfolding" is like that of "meanest insects on obscurest leaves," even if he is only "the brazen rod that stirs the fire/Because it must." (III, VII, ix, 521) If this censure seems unjust, as logically it may, perhaps it represents Hardy's dislike for dictators. After all, Hardy presents moments of "equilibrium" in Napoleon's career when he could have chosen peace; the Spirit of the Pities whispers to him on various occasions, in vain.

Napoleon knows that he is servant of the Will. Throughout the drama he feels that some conscious purpose of his own is checked

8. *Ibid.*, I, 63.

NAPOLEON

by an irresistible force inside himself. When Queen Louisa of Prussia begs Napoleon for mercy, Napoleon is touched, but he feels the urgency of the Will and says:

> Know you, my Fair,
> That I—ay, I—in this deserve your pity.—
> Some force within me, baffling mine intent,
> Harries me onward, whether I will or no.
> My star, my star is what's to blame—not I.
> (II, I, viii, 179)

He is momentarily touched by Josephine's tears at his decision to divorce her, but he hardens and states the doctrine of the Will: "We are but thistle-globes on Heaven's high gales,/And whither blown, or when, or how, or why,/Can choose us not at all!" (I, II, vi, 204) Again, just after the Spirit of the Years has exhibited "the films or brain-tissues of the Immanent Will, that pervade all things . . . NAPOLEON included," Napoleon speaks of Its operation: "Since Lodi Bridge/The force I then felt move me moves me on/Whether I will or no." (III, I, i, 330) He feels It, operating through the elements, move him to disaster. After he returns to Paris from the venture into Russia, he says:

> I have been subdued;
> But by the elements; and them alone.
> Not Russia, but God's sky has conquered me!

> . . . .
> The Genius who outshapes my destinies
> Did all the rest! (III, I, xii, 363)

Napoleon is not allowed to escape his destiny. He attempts suicide by taking poison before he goes to Elba, but is discovered and made to vomit before the poison takes effect. He says, "Fate has resolved what man could not resolve./ I must live on, and wait what Heaven may send!" (III, IV, iv, 415) He holds it unjust that he should be blamed for the corpses of his battlefields—or even made to think of them. When he sees them in a dream, he cries out: "Why, why should this reproach be dealt me now?/Why hold me my own master, if I be/ Ruled by the pitiless Planet of Destiny?" (III, VI, iii, 468) When the Spirit of the Years rebukes him after Waterloo, Napoleon says, "Yet, 'tis true, I have ever known/That such a Will I passively obeyed!" (III, VII, ix, 519)

His "Genius" inspires his stratagems. General Mack complains at Ulm that "The accursèd cunning of our adversary/Confounds all codes of honourable war," for Napoleon, instead of reaching Ulm through the Schwarzwald, "must wind/And corkscrew meanly round, where foot of man/Can scarce find pathway, stealing up to us/Thiefwise, by our back door!" (I, IV, iii, 69) Napoleon apparently foresees and prepares for all eventualities. Upon learning that Villeneuve has failed to support his intended attack upon England—a disobedience "scarce thinkable"—Napoleon immediately changes his plan to another he has already prepared. He says, "Foreseeing such might shape,/Each high- and by-way to the Danube hence/I have of late had measured, mapped, and judged." (I, III, i, 61) In this foresight, he acts as if taught by knowledge beyond common reason.

But Napoleon's inspiration only enables him to see manifold possibilities and, like water running down a slope, to find unerringly the channel of most immediate advantage. Piqued when Alexander of Russia delays in offering him the hand of Anne, Napoleon decides to wed Maria Louisa of Austria. Schwarzenberg, the Austrian ambassador, sees that Napoleon's "affront" will "thrust a thorn in Russia's side." Champagny, Napoleon's foreign minister, regards Napoleon's impulse to marry Maria Louisa, whom Napoleon has never seen[9] but has heard called "a bright blond thing," as a "scurrying dream." But when the impulse comes, Napoleon "unceremoniously" takes Madame Metternich's arm and tells her to consult the Austrian ambassador "Now, here, to-

9. Or "but barely." (II, V, vii, 285)

night." (II, V, i-ii, 263-264) Napoleon's inspiration from the Will impels him into the immediate channel. Obstructions farther on that reflective eyes foresee seem a part of the Will's design for churning Europe to a pulp.[10] Napoleon's impulses lead him to immediate successes. His ultimate defeat resembles, say, the defeat of the dinosaur that developed terrible jaws of immediate advantage, but neglected to develop brain.

The way Napoleon's inspirations come is described by the Spirit of Rumour. Napoleon draws his "Berlin Decree" from the non-reflective part of his mind. The Spirit says: "Maybe he meditates its scheme in sleep,/Or hints it to his suite, or syllables it/While shaping, to his scribes." (II, I, vi, 166) This is the method of the Will, even in Its action upon Wellington, who acts "while discovering his intention to act." (III, VII, vii, 505)

Napoleon, serving the Will, regards himself as above man-made laws and institutions. When he is to be crowned Emperor, he takes the crown from the altar himself, instead of re-

---

10. Such spontaneous reaction to impulses from the Will is in accordance with the theories of parapsychology. Experiments show that persons subject to psychic influences are most clairvoyant when they choose without reflection. As Rhine says, taking thought "In some instances . . . distorts the psi process so that psi-missing or the avoidance of the target takes place." Rhine, p. 123.

ceiving it from the archbishop, and places it on his own head. At least under the circumstances given in Hardy's play, it is clear that in returning from Elba, Napoleon, as Castlereagh charged, "stepped upon the only pedestal/On which he cares to stand—his lawless will." (III, V, v, 444)

To his nation, Napoleon is something like a major domo: as he is servant to the Will that thrusts him crassly and without feeling, so are his followers to him, fascinated pawns of his will in a game for empire. He boasts of his peculiarly magnetic power to General Mack, saying: "Two hundred thousand volunteers, right fit,/Will join my standards at a single nod," in comparison with Mack's Austrian "recruits, compulsion's scavengings." (I, IV, v, 75-76) His navy was defeated at Trafalgar because he was not there: "Well, well; I can't be everywhere!" A Chorus of the Pities marvels at his "Strange suasive pull of personality!" An Ironic Chorus answers that "His projects they unknow, his grin unsee!" and a Chorus of the Pities agrees that Napoleon is able to dupe his soldiers because "Their loyal luckless hearts say blindly—He!" (I, VI, i, 110-113) This blind loyalty is loyalty to the man in person, not to the office or the nation. Furthermore, the French feel it as a compulsive power only when

Napoleon is serving the Will, driving ahead in the lust of power and command. When he is not present in person or when he is defeated or despondent, so that the drive of the Will is impeded, loyalty wanes. Napoleon's palace servants bring out their white cockades after Napoleon has fled to Fontainebleau and the Allies approach Paris. A servant says, "And to cap all, the people of Paris are glad of the change. They have put a rope round the neck of the statue of Napoleon on the column of the Grand Army, and are amusing themselves with twitching it and crying 'Strangle the tyrant!'" (III, IV, iii, 408) Napoleon does not care what happens when he has abdicated and is being taken to Elba: "I'll mount the white cockade if they invite me!/. . . . all is lost in Europe for me now!" When he is in this mood, the people of Avignon howl at him: "Is that the Corsican? No; where is he? Give him up; give him up. We'll pitch him into the Rhone!" (III, IV, vi, 418-420)

But when the Will again stirs the lust for power in Napoleon, the pull of his person again sways men out of reason. Napoleon returns from Elba, and French royalist regiments are sent to capture him. Napoleon sends a detachment under an aide to "parley on Napoleon's behalf," and the royalist soldiers are ready to fire on this rebel band. Then Napoleon rides up, "his well-known profile keen against the hills," dismounts, and steps forward. The royalist officer, Lessard, orders his men to level their guns at Napoleon, but Napoleon still advances, saying:

> Men of the Fifth,
> See—here I am! . . . Old friends, do you not know me?
> If there be one among you who would slay
> His Chief of proud past years, let him come on
> And do it now.

Lessard remarks, "They are death-white at his words!/They'll fire not on this man. And I am helpless." The soldiers burst out: "Why yes! We know you, father. Glad to see ye!/ The Emperor for ever!" A grenadier says, "Yes, verily, sire./You are the Angel of the Lord to us;/We'll march with you to death or victory!" (III, V, iii, 435-437) Marshall Ney was sent to take Napoleon, but in the man's presence "flung his arms round his neck and joined him with all his men." (III, V, vi, 451-452) That Ney, admirable in so many ways, should be so hypnotized by Napoleon puzzles the Spirit of the Pities, who, regarding this "Simple and single-souled lieutenant," says, "Why should men's many-valued motions take/ So barbarous a groove!" (III, VII, iv, 497)

No one answers him, for his Chorus had answered him in observing Napoleon's "Strange suasive pull of personality!"

As servant of the Will, Napoleon is pitiless. To representations that fever raged on Villeneuve's ships and Villeneuve feared "unparalleled disaster," Napoleon calls his admiral "a wretched moral coward,/. . . this rank incompetent, this traitor—/Of whom I asked no more than fight and lose." (I, III, i, 57-58) He orders his soldiers at Austerlitz to "Maintain the ranks;/ Let none be thinned by impulse or excuse/Of bearing back the wounded." (I, VI, i, 110) He orders cannon to smash the ice on Satschan lake across which the already defeated Russians are fleeing. The soldiers of his Grand Army in Russia plod on through the snows, but Napoleon abandons them. The news breaks their spirit: "Other soldiers spring up as they realize the news, and stamp hither and thither, impotent with rage, grief, and despair . . . sobbing like children." (III, I, xi, 358) But when Napoleon gets to Paris, he makes a joke of his "ridiculous" defeat. Marie Louise tries to make him see the horror of it:

> But those six hundred thousand throbbing throats
> That cheered me deaf at Dresden, marching east

So full of youth and spirits—all bleached
bones—
Ridiculous? Can it be so, dear, to—
Their mothers, say?

Napoleon has a "twitch of displeasure" at this point of view and says, "I meant the enterprise and not its stuff." His concern for the "stuff" is clear in his immediate resolve to raise another army of three hundred thousand men to fight in Spain, for "Fishes as good/Swim in the sea as have come out of it." (III, I, xii, 363-364)

Though reported agreeable in domestic life when he has his way, Napoleon can be callous in personal relations. He is pitiless toward Josephine. When he commands her not only to agree to a divorce, but to help him win Maria Louisa for his bride, she says, "It is the— last humiliating blow!—/I cannot—O, I will not!" Napoleon replies fiercely, "But you *shall*!/And from your past experience you may know/That what I say I mean!" (II, V, ii, 262) He ordered the citizens of Soissons to prepare ceremonies for his meeting with Marie Louise, but he rides to meet her at Courcelles. He is only amused at their discomfiture: "How we have dished the Soissons folk, with their pavilions, and purple and gold hangings for the bride and bridegroom to meet in, and stately ceremonial to match, and their thousands looking on! Here we are where there's nobody. Ha, ha!" (II, V, vi, 279)

Like the Will, Napoleon is amoral. The only value in his morality (with one exception discussed below) is himself. Napoleon has already lost the battle of Waterloo when he sees the Prussians under Blücher coming in for the *coup de grace*. Without a thought for the lives of his men, Napoleon proposes to tell them the coming army is Grouchy's thirty-three thousand reinforcements. Ney objects "indignantly that such a feint/Is not war-worthy." Napoleon scowls, takes snuff, and sends his messengers to spread the hopeless, merciless lie. At this the Spirit Sinister praises him for "being without a conscience." (III, VII, viii, 510-511)

Napoleon accepts with pleasure homage that implies him to be a god. The President of the Senate congratulates Napoleon on the birth of a son, which is "The advent of this New Messiah, sire." Napoleon is evidently pleased as he replies, "You might have drawn the line at the Messiah./But I excuse you." (II, VI, iii, 296) At Borodino, Napoleon's officers please him by placing a portrait of his son within his tent. The boy is pictured as "playing at cup-and-ball, the ball being represented as the globe." Napoleon puts the portrait on a chair and commands his soldiers to march past this icon; they do so, cheering "The Emperor and the King of Rome for ever!" To underscore the meaning of this scene, Hardy has Napoleon observe the Russian clergy bear the Christian image through the ranks. Napoleon remarks cynically:

> Ay! Not content to stand on their own
>   strength,
> They try to hire the enginry of Heaven.
> I am no theologian, but I laugh
> That men can be so grossly logicless,
> When war, defensive or aggressive either,
> Is in its essence Pagan, and opposed
> To the whole gist of Christianity!
>   (III, I, iv, 342)

But that war is pagan does not bother Napoleon. In fact, he says bitterly, in his defeat, that he had hoped to replace Christ: "To shoulder Christ from out the topmost niche/In human fame, as once I fondly felt,/Was not for me." (III, VII, ix, 520)

When Napoleon is defeated, he always blames someone else. He blames the defeat at Salamanca on Marmont's daring to fight without orders: "Why gave he battle without biddance, pray,/From the supreme commander? Here's the crime/Of insubordination, root of woes!"

(III, I, iv, 341) As Moscow burns, Napoleon says:

> May Heaven curse the author of this war—
> Ay, him, that Russian minister, self-sold
> To England, who fomented it.—'Twas he
> Dragged Alexander into it, and me!

The statement is so outrageous that "The marshals are silent with looks of incredulity, and Caulaincourt shrugs his shoulders." (III, I, viii, 351) At Leipzig, Napoleon charges all his generals with "scopeless apathy," saying, "Except me, all are slack!" He turns especially to Murat and charges him without basis with "inclining to abandon me!" He regrets that he gave Murat a kingdom, for "as full monarch, you have foraged rather/For your own pot than mine!" Again, the charges are so outrageous that "MURAT and the marshals are silent, and look at each other with troubled countenances." (III, III, i, 380-381) As Wellington remarks when Ney charges recklessly at Waterloo, "I know Napoleon. If the onset fail/It will be Ney's; if it succeed he'll claim it!" (III, VII, iv, 495)

But at moments the Will in Napoleon fails to move him with his usual spring. When he is in good spirits and victorious, he sees the world only as a chessboard on which to play his brilliant game. But when he suffers, so that his thrust for power is impeded by his reluctant body, the sights he has seen emerge from his subconsciousness as shapes of horror.

Hardy may have worked out this process from suggestions in the *Philosophy of the Unconscious*. "The Unconscious," said Von Hartmann, "usually always calls forth as a motive in the brain *the reaction which is the easiest.*"[11] When Napoleon is in fine fettle, his easiest reaction is to thrust aside any question of costs (in human life or otherwise) and to drive on toward power and command. *"The Unconscious does not grow weary,* but all conscious mental activity becomes fatigued, because its material organs become temporarily unserviceable, in consequence of a quicker consumption of material than nutrition can repair in the same time."[12] As the impulses of the Unconscious must be put into action through the human brain acting as mechanism, the Will is impeded when this mechanism is fatigued. "Nervous fatigue increases the repugnance to pain, diminishes the effort to retain pleasure; thus increases the pain of pain, diminishes the pleasure in pleasure."[13] The drive of the Will in Napoleon as a lust for power promises the

11. Von Hartmann, II, 347.   12. *Ibid.*, II, 47.
13. *Ibid.*, III, 73.

pleasure of triumph. Fatigue increases the pain of effort and dulls the exuberance of the leap toward victory. Weary or ill, Napoleon lacks the vigor he needs to respond to the Will, as an athlete weary or ill may lack the stamina to respond to the cheers that urge him on. Von Hartmann suggested that oppressive feelings thrust into the subconscious emerge in weariness or sleep: "Before falling asleep, when the intellect becomes weary, the feelings which oppress us emerge the more powerfully because they are not impeded by thoughts."[14] Certainly Napoleon saw the spectacles of suffering spread before his eyes on his battlefields, but under the spell of the Will thrust feeling of their horror into his subconsciousness. Under the conditions Von Hartmann stated, they emerge.

In accordance with these suggestions, Hardy traces the forces that impede Napoleon's genius through stages of physical deterioration, weariness, and sleep.

Details of Napoleon's physical deterioration —his growing stoutness, his pallor, his colds in the head—are cited in the discussion of the Will in Chapter Three. We may recall especially Napoleon's illness at the battle of Borodino. There, as he coughs, sips his grog, and blinks upon the battle that he says will be another

14. *Ibid.*, II, 48.

"sun of Austerlitz," something more happens to him than the failure of the Mind to show him the way to victory. The Spirit of the Pities comments: "The ugly horror grossly regnant here/Wakes even the drowsed half-drunken Dictator/To all its vain uncouthness!" But Napoleon is waked only to awareness, not moved to pity. Deserted by inspiration for maneuvering, he only "orders a still stronger attack on the great redoubt in the center." (III, I, v, 344)

The same section of Chapter Three discusses Napoleon's weariness and despondency in defeat as an impediment to the Will. On the way to Elba, Napoleon concludes that "all is lost in Europe for me now!" But the Will does not relax, and after a while an impulse stirs the flaccid brain: "after some moments," Napoleon says: "But Asia waits a man,/And— who can tell?" (III, IV, vi, 420) It is interesting that Hardy added "after some moments" in revision.[15] The addition sharpens the idea that the Will can scarcely move Napoleon in this despondent mood, but keeps suggesting until he reacts.

After the swoop through France, Napoleon falls asleep while reviewing his troops. When he wakes his "listless eye" falls upon the Decla-

15. See American edition, p. 169.

ration of the Allies that he is "an enemy and disturber of the tranquillity of the world" and has "rendered himself liable to public vengeance." In the listlessness induced by sleep, the lust for power is checked, and Napoleon is for a moment, if not remorseful, at least frightened: "His flesh quivers, and he turns with a start, as if fancying that some one may be about to stab him in the back." (III, VI, i, 454) This fear prepares for the horror with which he soon afterward dreams of the corpses on his battlefields, as presented by the Duke of Enghien. But even horror does not move him to compassion and active resistance to the Will; it moves him only to lay the blame for his behavior on "the pitiless Planet of Destiny." In the wood of Bossu, Napoleon's "head droops lower and lower as he sits listless in the saddle, and he falls into a fitful sleep." This prepares him for the "spectral questionings" of the Spirits. They bring him to awareness that his lust for power has made Europe a shambles and earned him an insect's place in the drama of "Earth's unfolding." (III, VII, ix, 519-521) But it is only awareness that stirs Napoleon, even in Bossu. He has "passively obeyed" the Will too long to feel compassion now.

Perhaps Hardy disliked Napoleon particularly because he usurped the French Revolution and used its fervor to gratify his lust for power. Hardy picks up Napoleon's career only after this lust has begun to rule him. *The Dynasts* indicates that when Napoleon was young he had felt unselfishly and that he retained the capacity to feel so in some situations, especially those concerned with women. Seeming to reflect Von Hartmann's thought that the "passion for commanding and ruling" necessarily stifles liberty, and that power "is possible only at the expense of infringing . . . the impulse for liberty, in the ruled,"[16] the Spirit of the Pities states what had happened to Napoleon. He was born with great powers; he had "large potencies/Instilled into his idiosyncrasy," and he at first used these potencies "To throne fair Liberty in Privilege'[s] room." But his powers took taint, and Napoleon's unselfish feeling sank "to common plots/For his own gain." (Fore Scene, p. 3)

Continuing to brood upon Napoleon's apostasy, the Spirit observes him seat himself on the throne in Milan to receive the Italian sceptre. This is the man, he recalls, who "Professed at first to flout antiquity,/Scorn limp conventions, smile at mouldy thrones,/And level dynasts down to journeymen!—" When Napoleon places the crown upon his own head, the

16. Von Hartmann, III, 56.

Spirit of the Pities can hold his peace no longer. He throws a whisper into Napoleon's ear:

> Lieutenant Bonaparte,
> Would it not seemlier be to shut thy heart
> To these unhealthy splendours?—helmet thee
> For her thou swar'st-to first, fair Liberty?

This whisper reminds Napoleon that when he was mere "Lieutenant" he had fought for freedom and was free of the lust for power. The whisper is so clear that Napoleon asks, "Who spoke to me?" But in the grip of the Will—as the Spirit of the Years points out—the crown upon his head, Napoleon dismisses the suggestion as "aggressive Fancy, working spells/Upon a mind o'erwrought!"[17]   (I, I, vi, 33-36)

Some feeling of pity almost moves Napoleon when the beautiful, gallant Queen Louisa of Prussia accepts a rose he gives her and "with waiting tears" says, "Let Magdeburg come with it, sire! O yes!" At least Napoleon is touched enough that, like a reluctant servant carrying out an ugly order, he blames the Master: "My star, my star is what's to blame—not I." Heartbroken, Queen Louisa goes away. In a speech that suggests in his character a mixture of vul-

17. In the first version "helmet thee/For her thou swar'st-to first" reads "render thee/To whom thou swarest first." (American edition, p. 56.) The change suggests Hardy's intention to portray the Spirit of the Pities as more aggressive; the Spirit would have Napoleon fight for liberty.

garity, a bully's triumph, and some shame, Napoleon says to Talleyrand: "She was within an ace of getting over me. As she stepped into the carriage she said in her pretty way, 'O I have been cruelly deceived by you!' And when she sank down inside, not knowing I heard, she burst into sobs fit to move a statue. The Devil take me if I hadn't a good mind to stop the horses, jump in, give her a good kissing, and agree to all she wanted." But Napoleon is no statue to be melted by sobs, and he concludes, "I have kept in my right mind." (II, I, viii, 178-179)

Once in the drama, Napoleon does feel pity and act upon the feeling, with astounding results. This occasion, when Marie Louise gives birth to Napoleon's son, is discussed in the presentation of the Will in Chapter Three. That "The Will grew conscious at command" is an instance of a "fair desire" that bends "a digit the poise of forces." The lines suggest that human feeling may inform the Mind and influence It, at least in the area of impulses that lie at the source of life. At any rate, the occasion is the only one in the play where Napoleon is portrayed as sacrificing self for loving-kindness's sake.

The workings of the Will in Napoleon particularly are emphasized throughout *The Dy-*

nasts. Though others speak of strange warnings and hear the words of the Spirits, Napoleon is the only human character distinctly aware that he serves the Will. Its impulses fan out through him as Its major domo. He exercises a personal, compelling power like Its own, over most of the people of France. In turn, if not in gratitude, the Will serves Napoleon well. It throws Mack in agitation at Ulm; It causes General Weirother "impatiently" to say "Pah!" to the objections of his generals and to abandon the hill-positions at Austerlitz. (I, VI, ii, 114-115) It sends Napoleon's would-be assassin to the honorable Fox; It beguiles the foolish Russian Alexander; and above all, It enchants men like Ney and, indeed, the whole French nation after Elba. It works also in Napoleon's enemies, the English. Hardy makes the point, in the final display of the Will, that It manipulates "WELLINGTON in its tissue with the rest." But it would seem that a force opposite to this impulsive Will also, to some extent, informs Wellington. Napoleon's egoistic genius trusts no one's wisdom but his own. He tells Decrès to make "no question of one jot" in his orders, (I, I, ii, 13) and finds it "scarce thinkable" that Villeneuve should disobey unreasonable commands. (I, II, iii, 44) Wellington lacks Napoleon's genius, but trusts his officers. He has a general plan at Victoria, "But much and wide discretionary power/Is left the generals all." (III, II, i, 365) In short, though the Will is the Back of Things and pulls all the halyards of the world, there is an area that Hardy called equilibrium. Most men feel, rightly according to Hardy's letters, some leeway.

Just as any man, made aware through his senses, has some freedom to resist the Will, so here and there, even in France, sensitive men resist Napoleon. Villeneuve is such a man, a patriot who "would yield the heel-drops of his heart/With joyful readiness this day, this hour,/To do his country service"—but his concept of country includes his common sailors as his fellowmen. (I, III, i, 58) Beyond this, he has some humane feeling for even the enemy. In the hottest of the fire at Trafalgar, he says, "How hideous are the waves, so pure this dawn! —/Red-frothed; and friends and foes all mixed therein." (I, V, iii, 91) His inner conflict when he has disobeyed Napoleon may symbolize mankind's ultimate difficulty in resisting the Will, for it must always seem that "An Emperor's chide is a command to die." (I, V, vi, 104)

England is the victor in the war with Napoleon, and in the larger allegory England stands (along with the Spirit of the Pities) for mankind. The English leaders are not without their faults, but in general they oppose to Napoleon's lust for power their unselfish love of country. Pitt, "Frail though and spent, and an-hungered for restfulness," exhausts himself for the nation. (I, I, iii, 17) Not jealous of power, he pleads with the King to add to his ministry "brilliant intellects of the other side" to unify the country. (I, IV, i, 66) His dying words are "My country! How I leave my country!" (I, VI, viii, 136) As Nelson dies, he speaks with compassion of the man who shot him, and was shot. As Sir John Moore dies at Coruña, his chief interest is in the battle, and when he hears that the English advance, he says, " 'Tis *this* way I have wished to die!" (II, III, iii, 221) Fox dies of overwork for his country, and the Spirit of the Pities says of him, "He was the friend of peace—did his great best/ To shed her balms upon humanity." (II, I, ii, 152) Hardy does not entirely approve of Wellington, who is less generous than the others; he has the Spirit Ironic comment that Wellington does nothing to save the gallant, misguided Ney from "ignominious death." (III, VII, iv, 496) But Wellington too serves his country rather than himself.

When Napoleon is considered a human analogue of the Will, and those who oppose him types of men opposed to Its world-order, the historical drama partly illustrates the process by which consciousness may wake the Mind. Dynasts arise from century to century and enchant the nations. But also in stolid masses "The pale pathetic peoples still plod on/ Through hoodwinkings to light!" (III, IV, iv, 414) The people's hope is that of the Prussians after Jena; they must endure "till desperateness/Sting and excite a bonded last resistance,/And work its own release." (I, I, vi, 163)

But the peoples are dull in the main; Hardy does not suggest otherwise. Perhaps they cannot alone ever see through the hoodwinkings. Napoleon is conquered only when "the dull peoples and the Dynasts both" overthrow him. (III, VII, ix, 520) Then, on the Continent at least, "Europe's wormy dynasties rerobe/Themselves in their old gilt, to dazzle anew the globe!" (III, VII, viii, 518) The Shade of the Earth may well protest that downing one dynasty to set another up is objectless monotony. The play, suggesting that evolution is a long and intricate process, does not fully treat this problem, but perhaps a solution may be inferred. Napoleon makes one wholly generous decision, to have the physician save Marie Louise rather than his heir. The Will immediately fulfils his desire. Perhaps, when men of genius who might be dynasts are informed by science, religion, and poetry, they may come gradually to choose the way of loving-kindness rather than power and fame. Then the Mind, taught by Its favored servants, may lend Its aid through incursions that generate and inspire yet other men of genius, in the course of ages raising the level of the race. Development of this kind seems implied by Hardy's faith in evolution.

Finally, with its apparent basis in the Christian principle of loving-kindness, Hardy's evolutionary meliorism has a strongly religious flavor. I think he meant it so. In his "Apology" for *Late Lyrics and Earlier* Hardy expresses the hope for "an alliance between religion, which must be retained unless the world is to perish, and complete rationality, which must come, unless the world also is to perish." He thought this alliance might be brought about by "the interfusing effect of poetry."[18] *The Dynasts* seems, among other things, an effort to fuse rational thought and religious feeling. Hardy believed the philosophers more rational than the creeds; he held the monist theory of the Will to be the most plausible explanation for the universe. In this theory, as Von Hartmann expressed it, the Will might

18. *Collected Poems*, p. 531.

develop consciousness and then find peace through annihilation. Hardy's feeling rejected this conclusion; in feeling he yearned for God. He fuses thought and feeling in the idea that the Will might evolve into God. This idea is more than the positivist's belief in man alone. Each man perishes in his generation, and an ever-selfish Will would forever raise up new dynasts.[19] Then the Will too must evolve, becoming God to guide man's evolution, or all is lost. When man can teach the Will to become God, He may in turn help man toward the Kingdom of God on earth.

19. The Spirit of the Pities defines the "Thee" that he hymns as "Who hurlest Dynasts from their thrones," a line for which Hardy gives the Greek of the "Magnificat," in a footnote. (After Scene, p. 522)

INDEX

Index

Persons, places, and subjects of minor importance and mentions are not indexed.

Alexander, 50, 78, 112, 141, 143, 188-9, 193, 202, 210
Archer, 4-5, 12-3, 21-3, 25, 70, 124, 128, 153, 174, 180-1
Austerlitz, 35, 55, 127, 130, 144, 184, 198, 205, 210

Borodino, 81, 83, 144, 148, 200, 204
Buchanan, *Drama of Kings*, 34-5, 37, 42-3, 53, 102n, 178, 186

Choruses, general, 33, 62, 92-3, 108, 114, 139, 181; sources of, 34-5, 37; as spokesmen for Hardy, 35-7, 37n, 38. *See* Spirits individually
Clairvoyance, 100, 125n, 126, 133, 134, 194n; defined, 128-9, 129n; instances, 131-2
Consciousness, in men, 15, 54, 83, 91-2, 101, 137-8, 155-7, 161-2, 165, 167, 169, 173, 179; in the Will, 26-7, 27n, 44n, 52, 62-3, 68, 70, 76, 83-4, 89, 92, 99-100, 103, 136-8, 150, 152-5, 157-60, 167-74, 176-9, 181, 209, 213-5; process of development, 26-7, 92, 137-8, 155-9, 167-9, 172-3; scientific support for development, 155, 171n
Cosmic Mind, 121, 124, 127, 127n, 136, 154, 169, 171n

Darwin, *Origin of Species*, 8, 10, 14, 17. *See* Evolution
Determinism, 2, 8, 16, 38-9, 48, 67, 88, 102-3, 109-10, 165, 167-8; of the Will, 101-3, 166-8. *See* Haeckel, and Spirits Ironic and Years

England, as symbol for mankind, 211-2
Evolution, 8, 35, 47, 67, 81, 91, 92, 101, 138-40, 156, 160, 167, 176, 178-9, 185, 213-5. *See* Darwin
Extra-sensory perception, 78, 125, 125n, 129. *See* Psychic phenomena

Fox, 45, 183, 210, 212
Freedom of the will, in the Spirits, 41, 43-4, 164; in men, 41, 48, 61, 91-2, 98, 161-7, 172, 211; in the Will, 161, 166-7. *See* Hardy, and Von Hartmann on

INDEX

Haeckel, *Riddle of the Universe*, 55, 110; monism of, 18-21; determinism of, 18, 47-8

Hardy, interest in psychic phenomena, vii, 2-7, 7n, 11-3, 22-4, 123-4 (*see* Psychic phenomena); reading of Von Hartmann, vii, 9-14, 16-7, 25, 27, 90-1, 124, 153-4; preparation for writing *The Dynasts*, vii, 13-4, 87, 89, 123; use of history, vii, 183-5, 207; *Dynasts*, editions used, viii, 14n, 44n, 97n; temperament, 2-3, 5-6, 7n, 8, 21, 29, 32-3, 42, 114, 123, 215; on supernatural and superstition, 2-4, 4n, 5, 5n, 6-7, 21-5, 121-3; general reading, 2, 8-10, 17, 37, 46, 107, 122, 168; exasperation with critics, 2, 28; as stoic, 2, 45-6, 52; "Thoughts of Phena," 3n; "Sign Seeker," 5-6; "Vagg Hollow," 5n; on rationalism, 6, 8, 27, 28, 214; speculations on reality, 6, 20n, 87; "Withered Arm," 7, 7n; *Woodlanders*, 7, 9, 88; "Hap," 8, 9; as sceptic, 8, 12, 16, 22-5, 124; religious attitude, 8, 16, 32, 154-5, 214-5; education of, 8, 17; reading of Schopenhauer, 9-10, 87-9, 154; intention in *The Dynasts*, 16-7, 25-6, 28-32, 86, 123, 182-5, 207, 208n, 211, 214; "Impercipient," 16n; "In Tenebris," 16n; "Panthera," 18, 18n; reading of Haeckel, 18, 47; as monist, 20, 20n, 24-5, 56, 76, 88, 124, 214; "God's Education," 21n, 170; reading of Buchanan, 34, 37, 186; *Tess of the D'Urbervilles*, 45-6; "Rome: The Vatican," 46; *Return of the Native*, 65, 110; on war, 70-1, 174; "He Wonders about Himself," 152-4; on suicide (annihilation), 160-1, 171, 174 (*see* Suicide); on freedom of the will, 162-6, 211 (*see* Freedom of the will); "Lacking Sense," 170; "There Seemed a Strangeness," 176n; "Apology," 180n, 214; "Agnostoi Theoi," 181, 181n

Immanent Will in *The Dynasts*, Hardy's concept of as Mind, vii, ix, 10-1, 20n, 21, 21n, 24, 41, 52, 88, 93-109, 114-6, 120-1, 127, 136-9, 148, 166-7, 169-71, 173-4, 177-9, 186; names for, ix, 92-5; purpose in, 16, 91, 100, 100n, 101-2, 105-7, 139-40, 167, 186, 194; in need of man's aid, 20n, 159-60, 168-71, 176-80, 214; processes and manipulations, 21, 24, 39-40, 72, 91, 96-103, 114-6, 128, 138-48, 161-2, 165-6, 176-81, 183, 185-9, 191, 194, 196, 203, 205, 210-1, 214; as fundamental energy, 21, 24, 89, 92, 109; displayed, 40, 83, 95-8, 111, 114, 116, 162, 191, 210; resisted, 54, 139, 148-51, 165, 206, 211-13; morality of, 62, 70, 75, 83, 103-5, 168-9, 174, 177-8, 200; responsibility for pain, 81, 83, 105; as outside space and time, 93, 107-9, 139, 166; as dreaming, 101-3, 166; impeded, 139, 142-8, 165, 196, 202-5; active in birth-processes, 178-80, 207, 209, 214

Instinct, 15-6, 106-7, 189-90

INDEX

Josephine, viii, 184, 191, 199

Life and non-life, unity of, 103, 110-4

Mack, 66, 141, 183, 190, 192, 195, 210
Maria Louisa (Marie Louise), 51, 59, 66, 111, 116, 118-20, 131, 134-5, 141, 146, 148-9, 193, 198-9, 209, 213
Meliorism, Hardy's belief in, 2, 11, 13, 25-7, 29, 36-7, 90, 170-2, 174, 178, 180-1, 214; claim to originality, 12, 26-7, 27n, 29, 152-4, 174-5; logic of, 26-7, 70, 83-4, 90, 92, 138, 154-5, 171-2, 175-7; defined, 29, 170-1, 176-8, 180; as evolutionary, 36, 87, 152-3, 156, 170, 172, 178, 180-1, 181n, 214; processes and stages of, 62, 83, 160-1, 172-8, 180, 188, 213-5
Mill, 8; concept of Mind, 10, 20n, 168

Napoleon, as servant of the Will, viii, 94, 97, 113-5, 141, 182-3, 186-98, 205-6, 208-10, 212; Years' judgment of, 49, 112, 183, 189-90, 192, 206; wedding of, 59, 66, 116-21, 131, 141, 193, 199; as selfish egoist, 74, 141, 182-3, 188, 201-2, 207-10; as pitiless, 74, 182, 184, 188, 191-2, 198-200, 208-9; as amoral and lawless, 74, 194-5, 200-1; coronation of, 75, 77, 79, 131, 140, 194, 207-8; lust for power, 75, 141, 182, 187-9, 196, 203, 206-8, 212; his son's birth, 89, 132, 136, 149, 179, 200, 209, 213; as boastful, 113, 190, 195, 202; as impulsive, 141-2, 193-4; deterioration of, 143-8, 196, 202-6; heritage of, 179, 207; various judgments of, 182-4, 195-6; Hardy's interpretation of, 182-6, 188, 206-7; divorce of, 184, 191, 199; metaphysical basis for, 185; magnetism of, 187, 195-8; attempted suicide, 192; concept of himself as god, 200-1; his son, 200-1
Nelson, 40, 104, 133, 141, 150-1, 212
Ney, 61, 146-7, 197, 200, 202, 210, 212

Pain, as flaw in cosmic process, 81, 83, 87, 103-4, 157-8, 171-2; as factor in consciousness, 103, 157-60, 172-3, 175-7, 203-4
Parapsychology, 121, 125, 127, 129, 165, 194n; defined, 125n, 179n
Pitt, 49, 50, 130, 183, 212
Prayer, 35, 55, 108, 154-5, 158, 161, 168, 172, 177, 180
Precognition, 122, 122n, 123, 125n, 126, 129; instances of, 4n, 40, 42, 60, 126n, 132-5, 142, 165-6; defined, 129n, 167
Psychic phenomena, 1-2, 12-3, 22, 91, 122-3, 125-6, 128, 179, 194n; instances of, 3, 4, 4n, 5, 5n, 120-1, 130-6, 142, 163, 187, 206, 208, 210; defined, 24, 125, 125n, 126n, 127n, 129, 186. *See* Clairvoyance, Precognition, Psychokinesis, and Telepathy, and Hardy, and Von Hartmann on
Psychokinesis, 126; instances of, 7, 7n, 135-6; defined, 129, 129n, 135

Recording Angels, 80, 86, 111

INDEX

Schopenhauer, *World as Will and Idea*, 88; concept of the Will, ix, 10, 88-9, 92, 107, 110, 148, 160, 166, 171; influence on *The Dynasts*, 9, 11, 16, 88, 170

Shade of the Earth, 58, 80, 92, 136; opinions, 81-2, 148, 157-8, 177, 213

Space and time, 107, 107n, 108, 127n

Spirit Ironic, choruses of, 35, 47, 55, 57, 66, 67, 69, 70, 75, 89-90, 101, 103, 138, 140, 149, 172, 195; learning of, 47, 55, 66-7; associated with Years and Pities, 47, 64-5, 69-70, 83-4; as logician, 54, 67-8, 84, 158, 173-4; opinions, 55, 59, 70-1, 79, 83-4, 101, 108, 139-40, 158, 168, 172, 195, 212; characterized, 65-6, 73; as Mercutio (jester), 65, 67, 69, 75, 108; as determinist, 67; as showman of human comedy, 68-9; as source of Causation, 70; as spokesman for Hardy, 71, 173-4, 212

Spirit of Rumour, as showman of events, 58, 79, 80, 86, 144, 194; communications with men, 68, 78-80, 131-2; power of prophecy, 78; as liar, 78-9; characterized, 78-9, 132; choruses of, 80; opinions, 80; as spokesman for Hardy, 86

Spirit of the Pities, choruses of, 35-6, 49, 57, 58, 62, 140, 155, 161, 172-3, 195, 198; as source of Causation, 41, 54, 131, 168, 176, 208; communications with men, 41, 60, 85, 130-1, 140-1, 163, 190, 208; as spokesman for Hardy, 42, 53, 62-3, 86, 161, 207, 212; inconsistency, 53-4, 61, 68, 85; characterized, 53-4, 63, 208n; as juvenile, 54-5, 57, 68, 85, 139, 176; opinions, 54, 57-8, 60-2, 67, 70, 79, 81-4, 97, 103-5, 108, 149, 155, 158, 161, 168, 172-3, 176, 178, 195, 197, 207-8, 212, 215n; as showman of suffering, 55-8, 86, 131, 161, 168, 176; as epic hero, 56; power of prophecy, 59-60; growth in stature of, 61, 68-9, 85, 176

Spirit of the Years, as spokesman for Hardy, 2, 39, 42, 44, 45, 52, 86; as stoic, 2, 44, 44n, 45, 52, 65, 175; as determinist, 16, 18, 41, 43-4, 47-8, 61, 67, 72, 114-5, 190, 208; choruses of, 35, 36, 48, 49, 58, 62, 77, 107; communications with men, 40, 46, 49, 85, 130-1, 133, 148-9, 163, 192; as channel of Causation, 41, 43, 133, 148-9, 163; as showman of the Will, 42-3, 45, 51, 83, 86, 96-101, 111, 114, 138, 143, 145, 191; learning of, 44, 46-7, 66-7; power of prophecy, 45, 50-1, 59-60, 134; opinions, 45-52, 58, 66-7, 69, 82-4, 103, 105, 155, 166, 168, 173

Spirit Sinister, as Iago (evil), 46, 72-5; characterized, 49, 71-5; chorus of, 58, 71, 75; Hardy's failure to develop, 71-3, 75-8; opinions, 71-4, 174, 200; as channel of Causation, 72, 75, 116-7, 119-20; communications with men, 75, 119-20

Spirits, communications with men, 1, 24, 38-40, 127-8, 206; as channels of Causation, 24, 32-4, 39-41, 95, 116, 119, 129, 132; clash of opinion among,

INDEX

29, 36-8, 41, 52, 54, 58-62, 68-9, 76, 80-6, 97, 151, 163; as spokesmen for Hardy, 30, 32, 33, 37-8, 42, 85, 85n, 86; defined, 30, 37-8, 41-2; as characters, 32, 33, 85, 85n, 86; as sources of Causation, 32, 33-4, 41; as spectators, 32, 37, 38, 41, 113, 132, 134-6, 148, 189; as impersonated abstractions, 32, 37, 95, 119; sources for, 34-5, 37, 39. *See* Spirits individually

Suicide (annihilation), of Villeneuve, 131, 148-9, 164; as desirable, 149, 160-1, 171; as goal of the Will, 159-60, 174, 215. *See* Hardy on

Superstition, defined, 124-5. *See* Hardy on

Talavera, 57, 68, 80, 173

Telepathy, 7, 124, 125n, 126; instances, 3, 23-4, 75, 120-1, 129-31; defined, 22-3, 129, 129n, 130

Trafalgar, 50, 130, 141, 150, 164, 195, 211

Ulm, 66, 112, 141, 192, 210

Villeneuve, 56, 85, 122n, 130-1, 140-1, 148-9, 161, 163-4, 188, 193, 198, 210, 211

Von Hartmann, concept of the Unconscious, ix, 10, 14-5, 26, 91-2, 98-101, 104, 107-10, 116, 128-9, 137, 148, 154-5, 157-60, 166-8, 171, 174, 178-9, 185-6, 203, 214-5; influence on Hardy summarized, 9-11, 14-6, 26, 153, 155; *Philosophy of the Unconscious* summarized, 14-5, 27; on freedom of the will, 15, 91-2, 162-3; as monist, 18-9, 20n; on growth of consciousness, 27, 62-3, 82, 84, 137-8, 155-60, 162, 169, 174-6, 178; on psychic phenomena, 91, 128-9, 132-4, 186; on suicide (annihilation), 159-60, 174, 215

Waterloo, 49, 58, 61, 68, 71, 74, 76, 80, 85, 112, 128, 142, 145-7, 166, 192, 200, 202

Wellington, 97, 147, 183, 194, 202, 210, 212

www.ingramcontent.com/pod-product-compliance
Lightning Source LLC
Chambersburg PA
CBHW021403290426
44108CB00010B/357